# STUDY GUIDE

# Weimar and Nazi Germany, 1918-39

Edexcel - GCSE

Published by Clever Lili Limited.

contact@cleverlili.com

First published 2020

ISBN 978-1-913887-02-5

Copyright notice

All rights reserved. No part of this publication may be reproduced in any form or by any means (including photocopying or storing it in any medium by electronic means and whether or not transiently or incidentally to some other use of this publication) with the written permission of the copyright owner. Applications for the copyright owner's written permission should be addressed to the publisher.

Clever Lili has made every effort to contact copyright holders for permission for the use of copyright material. We will be happy, upon notification, to rectify any errors or omissions and include any appropriate rectifications in future editions.

Cover by: Unknown author on Wikimedia Commons

Icons by: flaticon and freepik

Contributors: Lynn Harkin, Donna Garvey, Marcus Pailing

Edited by Paul Connolly and Rebecca Parsley

Design by Evgeni Veskov and Will Fox

All rights reserved

# DISCOVER MORE OF OUR GCSE HISTORY STUDY GUIDES
*GCSEHistory.com and Clever Lili*

    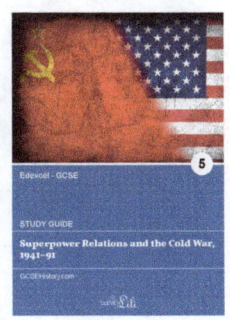 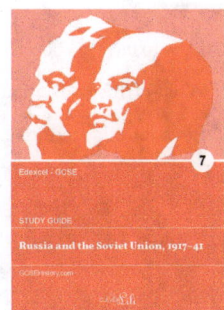

## THE GUIDES ARE EVEN BETTER WITH OUR GCSE/IGCSE HISTORY WEBSITE APP AND MOBILE APP

GCSE History is a text and voice web and mobile app that allows you to easily revise for your GCSE/IGCSE exams wherever you are - it's like having your own personal GCSE history tutor. Whether you're at home or on the bus, GCSE History provides you with thousands of convenient bite-sized facts to help you pass your exams with flying colours. We cover all topics - with more than 120,000 questions - across the Edexcel, AQA and CIE exam boards.

 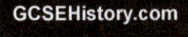  

# Contents

- How to use this book .................................................. 6
- What is this book about? ............................................. 7
- Revision suggestions .................................................. 9

## Timelines
- Weimar and Nazi Germany, 1918-1939 ............................. 13

## Origins of the Weimar Republic
- Impact of the First World War on Germany ....................... 16
- The German Revolution ............................................ 18
- Weimar Germany (including Parties) .............................. 18
- Treaty of Versailles, 1919 ........................................ 22

## Political Challenges, 1919 to 1922
- What Are Left-Wing Views? ........................................ 23
- What Are Right-Wing Views? ....................................... 24
- Political Challenges .............................................. 25
- Political Violence ................................................ 26
- Spartacist Revolt, 1919 .......................................... 27
- The Kapp Putsch, 1920 ............................................ 28

## Economic Challenges, 1923
- The Ruhr Crisis, 1923 ............................................ 29
- Hyperinflation, 1923 ............................................. 31

## Weimar Recovery, 1924 to 1929
- Dawes Plan, 1924 ................................................. 32
- Locarno Pact, 1925 ............................................... 33
- League of Nations, 1926 .......................................... 34
- Kellogg-Briand Pact, 1928 ........................................ 35
- Young Plan, 1929 ................................................. 36
- Fully Recovered? ................................................. 37
- Standard of Living in Weimar Germany ............................ 38

## Changes in Society, 1924 to 1929
- Social Changes for Women ......................................... 38
- Cultural Changes ................................................. 39
- New Objectivism .................................................. 41
- Modernism ........................................................ 41
- Expressionism .................................................... 41
- The Bauhaus Movement ............................................. 42

## The Early Nazi Party, 1919 to 1923
- The DAP .......................................................... 42
- The SA ........................................................... 43
- The Nazi Party ................................................... 44
- Munich Putsch, 1923 .............................................. 46

## The Lean Years, 1924 to 1929
- The Lean Years, 1924 to 1929 .................................... 48
- Bamberg Conference, 1926 ......................................... 49
- Why Was Support for the Nazis Low from 1924-1929? .............. 50

## Hitler's Rise to Power, 1930 to 1933
- The Great Depression, 1930s ..................................... 51
- Why Support the Nazis? ........................................... 52
- Election Results ................................................. 55
- Presidential Elections, 1932 .................................... 55
- How Did Hitler Become Chancellor? ............................... 56

## Creation of a Dictatorship, 1933 to 1934
- Reichstag Fire, Feb 1933 ........................................ 58
- Decree for the Protection of the People and the State, March 1933 ... 59
- March Elections, 1933 ........................................... 60
- Enabling Act, March 1933 ........................................ 61
- Creating a Dictatorship ......................................... 61
- The Night of the Long Knives, June 1934 ........................ 63

## The Nazi Police State
- The Police State ................................................. 64
- The SS ........................................................... 65
- The Gestapo ...................................................... 66
- The SD ........................................................... 66
- Concentration Camps .............................................. 67
- The Legal System ................................................. 68

## Controlling Religion
- Controlling Religion ............................................. 68
- Catholics ........................................................ 69
- The Concordat .................................................... 70
- The Reich Church ................................................. 71
- Protestants ...................................................... 71
- The Pastors' Emergency League ................................... 72

## Nazi Propaganda and Censorship
- Nazi Propaganda .................................................. 72
- The Press ........................................................ 73
- Rallies .......................................................... 74
- Sport ............................................................ 75
- Literature ....................................................... 75
- Music ............................................................ 76
- Culture .......................................................... 76
- Radio ............................................................ 77
- Film ............................................................. 78

*Quizzes, amazing exam preparation tools and more at GCSEHistory.com*

Art .................................................................................. 78

# Living in Nazi Germany, 1933 to 1939

Nazi Policies - Women ................................................... 79

Nazi Policies - Youth ...................................................... 80

Nazi Policies - Education ............................................... 82

Nazi Policies - Employment ........................................... 83

Nazi Policies - Labour Front .......................................... 84

Nazi Policies - Standard of Living ................................. 85

# Nazi Persecution of Minorities

Persecution of Minorities ............................................... 87

Persecution of Disabled People ..................................... 89

Persecution of Homosexuals ......................................... 89

Persecution of Roma ...................................................... 90

Persecution of Jews ........................................................ 91

Jewish Shop Boycott, April 1933 ................................... 91

The Nuremberg Laws, 1935 ........................................... 92

Kristallnacht, November 1938 ....................................... 93

# Opposition to the Nazis

Opposition to the Nazi Regime ..................................... 94

Swing Youth .................................................................... 95

Edelweiss Pirates ............................................................ 95

White Rose Group .......................................................... 96

# Key People in Weimar and Nazi Germany

Charles G Dawes ............................................................. 96

Anton Drexler .................................................................. 97

Friedrich Ebert ................................................................ 98

Joseph Goebbels ............................................................. 98

Rudolf Hess ..................................................................... 99

Reinhard Heydrich ......................................................... 100

Heinrich Himmler .......................................................... 100

President Paul von Hindenburg .................................... 101

Adolf Hitler ..................................................................... 102

Dr Wolfgang Kapp .......................................................... 104

Karl Liebknecht .............................................................. 104

General Ludendorff ........................................................ 105

Rosa Luxemburg ............................................................. 106

Franz von Papen ............................................................. 106

Ernst Röhm ..................................................................... 107

Philipp Scheidemann ..................................................... 108

General von Schleicher .................................................. 108

Gustav Stresemann ......................................................... 109

Kaiser Wilhelm II ............................................................ 110

Owen Young .................................................................... 111

Glossary ........................................................................... 112

Index ................................................................................ 116

# HOW TO USE THIS BOOK

In this study guide, you will see a series of icons, highlighted words and page references. The key below will help you quickly establish what these mean and where to go for more information.

## Icons

 WHAT questions cover the key events and themes.

 WHO questions cover the key people involved.

 WHEN questions cover the timings of key events.

 WHERE questions cover the locations of key moments.

 WHY questions cover the reasons behind key events.

 HOW questions take a closer look at the way in which events, situations and trends occur.

 IMPORTANCE questions take a closer look at the significance of events, situations, and recurrent trends and themes.

 DECISIONS questions take a closer look at choices made at events and situations during this era.

## Highlighted words

Abdicate - occasionally, you will see certain words highlighted within an answer. This means that, if you need it, you'll find an explanation of the word or phrase in the glossary which starts on **page 112**.

## Page references

**Tudor** *(p.7)* - occasionally, a certain subject within an answer is covered in more depth on a different page. If you'd like to learn more about it, you can go directly to the page indicated.

# WHAT IS THIS BOOK ABOUT?

Weimar and Nazi Germany, 1918 to 1939, is the modern depth study that focuses on the origins of the Weimar Republic, the challenges it faced and to what extent it overcame those challenges. The course also investigates why and how the Weimar Republic was dismantled by the Nazis and replaced by a Nazi dictatorship. You will focus on crucial events during this period, and study the different social, cultural, political, economic and military changes that occurred.

## Purpose
This study enables you to understand the complexities and challenges that the democratic Weimar Republic faced and how it was transformed into a one-party state under the leadership of the Nazis. You will investigate themes such as democracy, revolution, dictatorship, government, propaganda, censorship, economy and society. This course will enable you to develop the historical skills of causation and consequence, and encourage you to analyse and evaluate contemporary sources as well as interpretations of the time period.

## Topics
Weimar and Nazi Germany, 1918 to 1939 is split into 4 key topics:

- Topic 1 looks at the Weimar Republic between 1918 and 1929. You will study the origins of the new republic, the political and economic challenges it faced and to what extent it recovered between 1924 and 1929. You will also study how society changed during the 'Golden Years.'.
- Topic 2 looks at the early development of the Nazi Party, the failed Munich Beer Hall Putsch and how the Nazi Party was reorganised afterwards. You will also study the political developments during the Great Depression and why and how Hitler became chancellor of Germany.
- Topic 3 looks at how Hitler and the Nazis dismantled the Weimar democracy, piece by piece, and created a one party dictatorship. You will study the ways in which the Nazis tried to control the hearts and minds of the German people using propaganda and censorship to control all aspects of life.
- Topic 4 looks at life in Nazi Germany and the Nazi policies towards women, children, education and the unemployed. You will study how living standards changed. The persecution of different minorities will also be explored.

## Key Individuals
Some of the key individuals studied on this course include:

- Adolf Hitler.
- Friedrich Ebert.
- Paul von Hindenburg.
- Gustav Stresemann.
- Rosa Luxemburg.
- Wolfgang Kapp.

## Key Events
Some of the key events you will study on this course include:

- The effects of the Treaty of Versailles on Germany.
- The French and Belgian occupation of the Ruhr, 1923.
- The impact of the Great Depression on Germany.
- Hitler becoming chancellor.
- The creation of the Nazi police state and the setting up of the Gestapo.
- The establishment of the Hitler Youth and the League of German Maidens.
- The Nazi persecution of the Jews such as the Nuremberg Laws.

## Assessment
Weimar and Nazi Germany, 1918-1939 is paper 3 where you have a total of 1 hour and 20 minutes to complete. There will be 3 exam questions which will assess what you have learnt. Question 3 will be broken down into a, b, c and d. You answer all questions.

- Question 1 is worth 4 marks. This question will require you to make two inferences from a source that answers the question asked. You will need to support each inference with relevant detail from the source. This could be in the form of a quote, detail from a visual source or by paraphrasing what the source states.

## WHAT IS THIS BOOK ABOUT?

- Question 2 is worth 12 marks. This question will require you to explain why an event occurred. You need to identify three reasons, support each one with accurate and relevant factual detail that is precisely selected and then clearly explain how each cause made the event happen.

- Question 3a is worth 8 marks. This question asks you to explain how useful two sources are for a specific enquiry using the content of the source, the provenance of the source and your own contextual knowledge.

- Question 3b is worth 4 marks. This question asks you to identify the main difference in the views of two historical interpretations on a specific topic. You have to support the main difference with details from both interpretations.

- Question 3c is worth 4 marks. This question asks you to suggest one reason why the views of the two historical interpretations might be different. You have to support the main difference with details from both interpretations and you could can use the sources from question 3a to help you answer the question.

- Question 3d is worth 16 marks and an additional 4 marks for spelling, punctuation and grammar. This question asks you to explain how far you agree with one of the interpretations. In your explanation you have to evaluate both interpretations, using your own knowledge of the historical context to come to your conclusion.

# REVISION SUGGESTIONS

Revision! A dreaded word. Everyone knows it's coming, everyone knows how much it helps with your exam performance, and everyone struggles to get started! We know you want to do the best you can in your GCSEs, but schools aren't always clear on the best way to revise. This can leave students wondering:

- ✓ How should I plan my revision time?
- ✓ How can I beat procrastination?
- ✓ What methods should I use? Flash cards? Re-reading my notes? Highlighting?

Luckily, you no longer need to guess at the answers. Education researchers have looked at all the available revision studies, and the jury is in. They've come up with some key pointers on the best ways to revise, as well as some thoughts on popular revision methods that aren't so helpful. The next few pages will help you understand what we know about the best revision methods.

## How can I beat procrastination?

This is an age-old question, and it applies to adults as well! Have a look at our top three tips below.

### ◎ Reward yourself

When we think a task we have to do is going to be boring, hard or uncomfortable, we often put if off and do something more 'fun' instead. But we often don't really enjoy the 'fun' activity because we feel guilty about avoiding what we should be doing. Instead, get your work done and promise yourself a reward after you complete it. Whatever treat you choose will seem all the sweeter, and you'll feel proud for doing something you found difficult. Just do it!

### ◎ Just do it!

We tend to procrastinate when we think the task we have to do is going to be difficult or dull. The funny thing is, the most uncomfortable part is usually making ourselves sit down and start it in the first place. Once you begin, it's usually not nearly as bad as you anticipated.

### ◎ Pomodoro technique

The pomodoro technique helps you trick your brain by telling it you only have to focus for a short time. Set a timer for 20 minutes and focus that whole period on your revision. Turn off your phone, clear your desk, and work. At the end of the 20 minutes, you get to take a break for five. Then, do another 20 minutes. You'll usually find your rhythm and it becomes easier to carry on because it's only for a short, defined chunk of time.

## Spaced practice

We tend to arrange our revision into big blocks. For example, you might tell yourself: "This week I'll do all my revision for the Cold War, then next week I'll do the Medicine Through Time unit."

*Get our free app at GCSEHistory.com*

# REVISION SUGGESTIONS

This is called **massed practice**, because all revision for a single topic is done as one big mass.

But there's a better way! Try **spaced practice** instead. Instead of putting all revision sessions for one topic into a single block, space them out. See the example below for how it works.

This means planning ahead, rather than leaving revision to the last minute - but the evidence strongly suggests it's worth it. You'll remember much more from your revision if you use **spaced practice** rather than organising it into big blocks. Whichever method you choose, though, remember to reward yourself with breaks.

### Spaced practice (more effective):

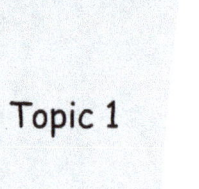

Massed practice (less effective)

# REVISION SUGGESTIONS

## What methods should I use to revise?

**Self-testing/flash cards**

**Self explanation/mind-mapping**

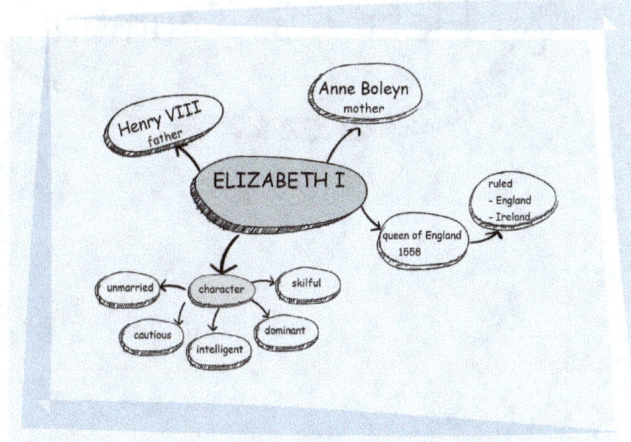

The research shows a clear winner for revision methods - **self-testing**. A good way to do this is with **flash cards**. Flash cards are really useful for helping you recall short – but important – pieces of information, like names and dates.

Side A - question

Side B - answer

Write questions on one side of the cards, and the answers on the back. This makes answering the questions and then testing yourself easy. Put all the cards you get right in a pile to one side, and only repeat the test with the ones you got wrong - this will force you to work on your weaker areas.

pile with right answers

pile with wrong answers

As this book has a quiz question structure itself, you can use it for this technique.

Another good revision method is **self-explanation**. This is where you explain how and why one piece of information from your course linked with another piece.

This can be done with **mind-maps,** where you draw the links and then write explanations for how they connect. For example, President Truman is connected with anti-communism because of the Truman Doctrine.

Get our free app at GCSEHistory.com

# REVISION SUGGESTIONS

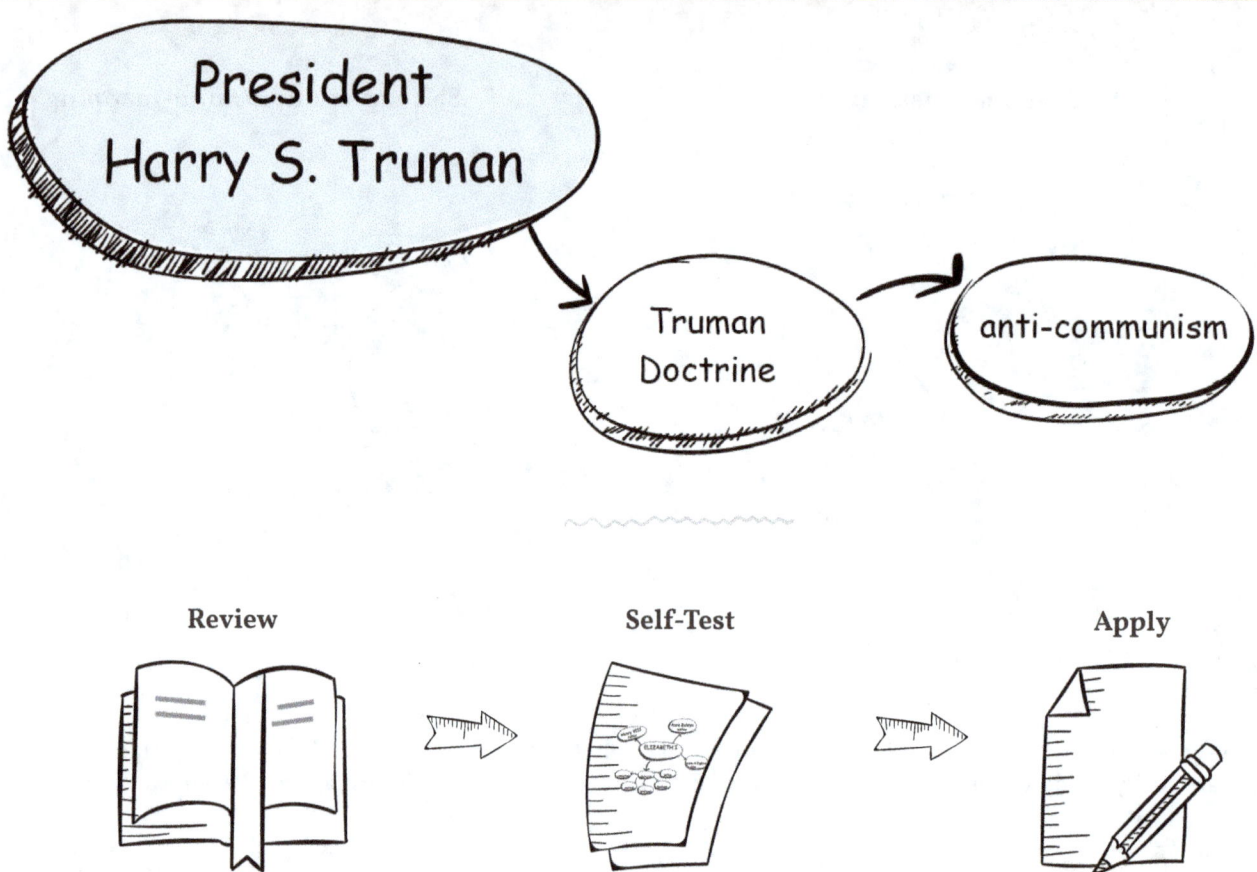

Start by highlighting or re-reading to create your flashcards for self-testing.

Test yourself with flash cards. Make mind maps to explain the concepts.

Apply your knowledge on practice exam questions.

## Which revision techniques should I be cautious about?

**Highlighting** and **re-reading** are not necessarily bad strategies - but the research does say they're less effective than flash cards and mind-maps.

If you do use these methods, make sure they are **the first step to creating flash cards**. Really engage with the material as you go, rather than switching to autopilot.

# WEIMAR AND NAZI GERMANY, 1918-1939

## TIMELINE

**1918**
- *9th November* - Kaiser Wilhelm II abdicated *(p.17)*
- *11th November* - Armistice signed *(p.17)*
- *November* - German Revolution

**1919**
- *5th January 1919* - Spartacist Uprising started *(p.27)*
- *February 1919* - German Workers' Party (DAP) founded *(p.42)*
- *28th June 1919* - Treaty of Versailles signed *(p.22)*
- *19th September 1919* - Hitler joined the DAP *(p.42)*

**1920**
- *February 1920* - Twenty-Five Point Programme published *(p.43)*
- *March 1920* - Kapp Putsch *(p.28)*

**1921**
- *July 1921* - Hitler became the leader of the NSDAP *(p.42)*

**1923**
- *January 1923* - Occupation of the Ruhr *(p.29)*
- *1923* - Hyperinflation crisis *(p.31)*
- *8th-9th November 1923* - Munich Beer Hall Putsch *(p.46)*

**1924**
- *April 1924* - Dawes Plan *(p.32)*

**1925**
- *April 1925* - SS set up *(p.65)*
- *December 1925* - Locarno Pact signed *(p.33)*

**1926**
- *February 1926* - Bamberg Conference *(p.49)*
- *September 1926* - Germany joined the League of Nations *(p.34)*

**1929**
- *August 1929* - Young Plan *(p.36)*
- *October 1929* - Wall Street Crash *(p.51)*

**1932**
- *March 1932* - Presidential Election *(p.56)*
- *May 1932* - Franz von Papen is appointed chancellor *(p.57)*
- *July 1932* - The Nazis won 230 seats *(p.55)*
- *December 1932* - General von Schleicher became chancellor *(p.57)*

**1933**
- *30th January 1933* - Hitler appointed chancellor of Germany *(p.56)*
- *27th February 1933* - Reichstag Fire *(p.58)*
- *March 1933* - March 1933 General Election *(p.60)*

# WEIMAR AND NAZI GERMANY, 1918-1939

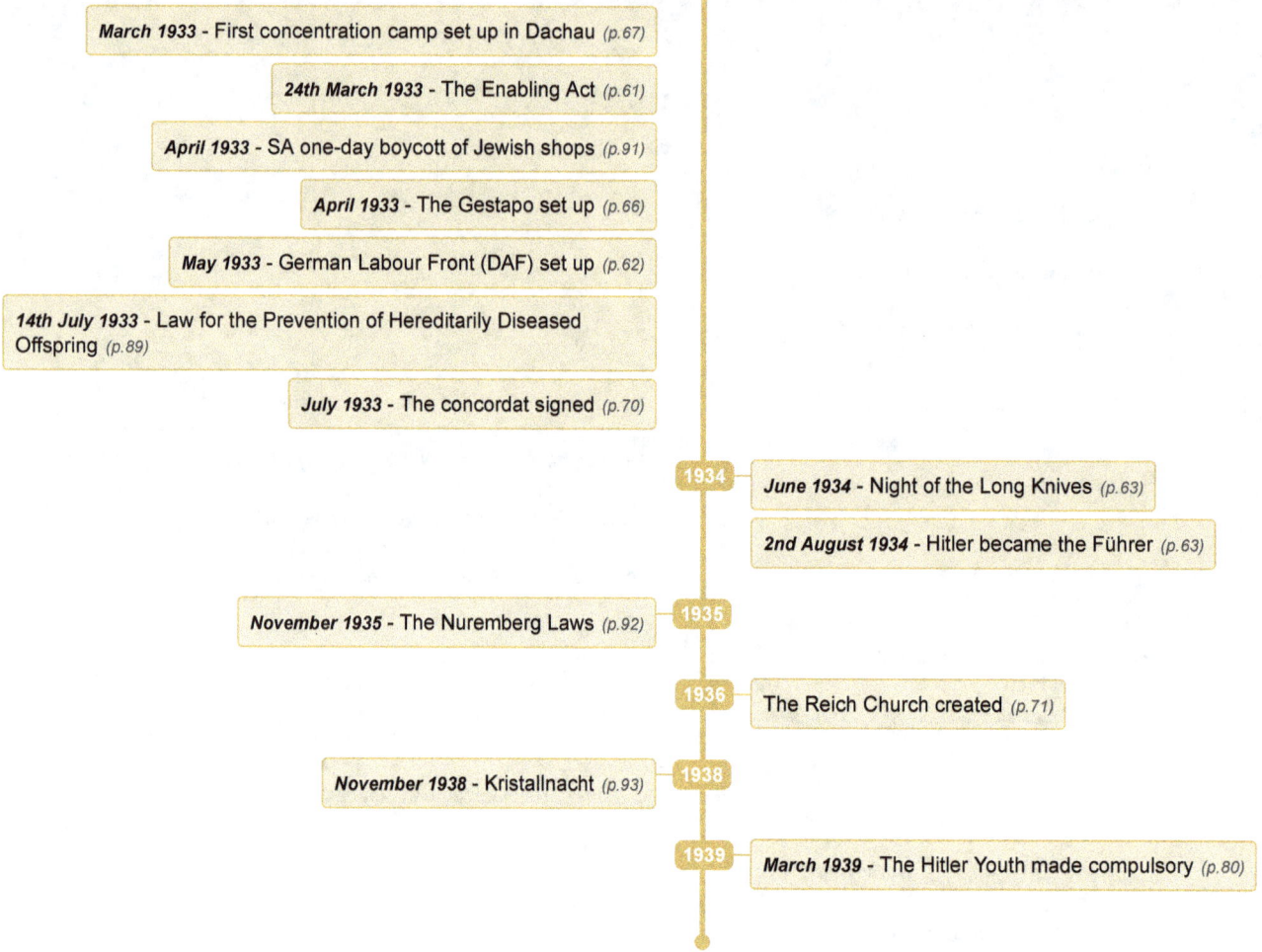

- **March 1933** - First concentration camp set up in Dachau *(p.67)*
- **24th March 1933** - The Enabling Act *(p.61)*
- **April 1933** - SA one-day boycott of Jewish shops *(p.91)*
- **April 1933** - The Gestapo set up *(p.66)*
- **May 1933** - German Labour Front (DAF) set up *(p.62)*
- **14th July 1933** - Law for the Prevention of Hereditarily Diseased Offspring *(p.89)*
- **July 1933** - The concordat signed *(p.70)*

**1934**
- **June 1934** - Night of the Long Knives *(p.63)*
- **2nd August 1934** - Hitler became the Führer *(p.63)*

**1935**
- **November 1935** - The Nuremberg Laws *(p.92)*

**1936**
- The Reich Church created *(p.71)*

**1938**
- **November 1938** - Kristallnacht *(p.93)*

**1939**
- **March 1939** - The Hitler Youth made compulsory *(p.80)*

# WEIMAR AND NAZI GERMANY, 1918-1939

# IMPACT OF THE FIRST WORLD WAR ON GERMANY

*The First World War had a huge impact on Germany.*

 **What happened with Germany and the First World War?**
The First World War had a huge impact on Germany's society, politics and economy.

 **How did Germany enter the First World War?**
The following 3 key events led to Germany entering the First World War.
- Germany declared war on Russia on the 1st August, 1914.
- After Germany invaded France via Belgium, Great Britain declared war on Germany on the 4th August.
- This was followed by the Ottoman Empire (Turkey) joining the war a few months later, in October, where it supported Germany.

 **How was Germany affected by the First World War?**
Germany was affected in 3 key ways:
- Germany was economically damaged and the country's debt increased to 150 billion marks.
- They were affected socially with two million troops and approximately 763,000 civilians dead.
- They were affected politically with many groups attempting to seize power, the Kaiser's abdication and Germany becoming a republic.

 **How did the First World War affect people socially in Germany?**
Germany was badly hit by the war because of the Allied Naval Blockade that stopped supplies getting into Germany during the war, and remained in place until the signing of the Treaty of Versailles, leaving many starving and ill.

 **How many casualties did the First World War claim in Germany?**
Germany was affected socially by the First World War in 5 key ways:
- They had a high casualty rate with approximately two million dead soldiers.
- Some 600,000 women were left as widows.
- The war also took its toll on civilians, with approximately 763,000 people dying from starvation.
- The gap between rich and poor had grown as a result of the war and increased social divisions.
- Over 1 and a half million soldiers returned home following the war, many struggling to adapt back to civilian life and accept defeat.

 **What happened to Germany's economy after the First World War?**
There were 7 significant negative effects on the economy:
- By 1918, industrial production was reduced by a third from 1913 levels.
- Fuel was short as a result of the war and consequently 300,000 people died from hypothermia.
- The government's budget was stretched by paying pensions to the 600,000 widows and 2 million orphans left after the war.
- Germany's debt was 50 billion German marks in 1914. This rapidly increased to 150 billion by 1918.
- Germany was bankrupt as it had spent all its gold reserves on the war.
- Inflation increased as a result of the weak German mark so the prices of goods were increasing.
- Germany was forced to begin interim payments to the Allies immediately after armistice was signed.

## What happened to Germany politically at the end of the First World War?

There were 5 important political effects:

- There was massive political unrest with uprisings and strikes, such as the naval mutiny in Kiel in October, 1918.
- The unrest spread to become the German Revolution *(p.18)* began, with huge consequences for the government and constitution of Germany.
- A communist state was declared in Bavaria on 7th November, 1918.
- The kaiser lost control and abdicated.
- The new Weimar Republic *(p.18)* was created, and by signing the Treaty of Versailles, was greatly resented by the German people.

## What were the events of the revolution in Germany before the end of the First World War?

There were 10 main events that occurred during the German Revolution *(p.18)*:

- The allies offered Germany an armistice to end the war. Part of their deal included that Germany become a democracy and the Kaiser should abdicate.
- The kaiser declined these terms, wishing to continue with the war.
- In response, the German Navy mutinied at the end of October 1918, refusing to follow the Kaiser's orders.
- Soon a domino effect occurred and by November 1918, there were demonstrations and strikes all across Germany and a communist state declared in Bavaria.
- On the advice of his government and the army, Kaiser Wilhelm abdicated on 9th November, 1918 and fled to the Netherlands.
- Philipp Scheidemann, a member of the Social Democratic Party (SPD), announced that Germany was a republic to prevent a communist government being declared on 9th November, 1918.
- Prince Max von Baden stepped down as the kaiser's chancellor. Friedrich Ebert, the leader of the SPD, took over as the chancellor of Germany.
- On 10th November, 1918, Ebert suspended the Reichstag (parliament) and formed the Council of People's Representatives to run the country until a new constitution was written.
- Germany signed a ceasefire or armistice with the Allies on 11th November, 1918 to end the fighting in the First World War.
- In January 1919, there were elections to the Constituent Assembly, or National Assembly, which would decide on the new constitution.

## What were the consequences of the German Revolution before the end of the First World War?

There were 3 key results of the German revolution *(p.18)*:

- The kaiser abdicated.
- Germany became a republic.
- This led to the end of the First World War.

### DID YOU KNOW?

The winter of 1916–1917 was known as the 'Turnip Winter' in Germany. Turnips were about the only food available to feed many people.

## THE GERMAN REVOLUTION

*Unrest quickly spread in Germany at the end of the First World War, leading to the collapse of the monarchy and a complete restructuring of the German government and constitution.*

### What was the German Revolution?
The German revolution was an uprising led by members of the navy, army and the workers who demanded peace negotiations to end the war in November 1918. This resulted in the collapse of the monarchy and the creation of a republic by January 1919.

### What was the German Revolution also known as?
The German Revolution of 1918 is sometimes called 'the November Revolution'.

### When was the German Revolution?
The German Revolution began after the Kiel Mutiny, at the end of October 1918, with a new republic established in January 1919. It is often called 'the November Revolution' because most of the key events occurred in that month.

### What caused the German Revolution?
The German revolution happened due to the economic problems of the war, war weariness and food shortages.

---

**DID YOU KNOW?**

Although the Armistice was signed in November 1918, the British blockade on Germany wasn't lifted until July 1919.

This meant that severe food shortages continued, and many Germans suffered from malnutrition and starvation.

---

## WEIMAR GERMANY (INCLUDING PARTIES)

*The Weimar Republic was the first time that Germany had a representative democracy.*

### What was the Weimar Republic?
Elected following the First World War, the Weimar Republic was Germany's first democratic government. The new government was formed in the town of Weimar, following the abdication of Kaiser Wilhelm II.

### When did the Weimar Republic exist?
The Weimar Republic existed from 1919 until 1933, when Hitler was appointed chancellor.

### Where was the Weimar Republic created?
Weimar was the town in central Germany where the constitutional assembly met to set up the new republic. It was too dangerous in Berlin, the capital, because of the unrest.

### What was the structure of the constitution of the Weimar Republic?
The political structure of the Weimar Republic was made up of four different elements:
- The president was the head of state.

- The chancellor was the head of government.
- The parliament which was divided into two houses, the Reichstag and the Reichsrat.
- The electorate was made up of all men and women aged 21 and over who were eligible to vote for the members of parliament.

## What was the role of the president in the Weimar Republic?

The president had many powers although they were limited:

- As head of state, the president did not take part in the day-to-day running of the country.
- He had the power to appoint and dismiss the chancellor.
- He could declare when Germany was at war and controlled the army, navy and airforce.
- He could use Article 48, under certain circumstances, to overrule his government and make emergency laws by decree if he deemed it necessary.
- He had to be elected every 7 years by the people.

## What was the role of the chancellor in the Weimar Republic?

The chancellor had many powers although they were limited:

- He was chosen by the president, usually from the political party that gained the most votes in the general election.
- As head of the government, he was responsible for the day-to-day running of the country.
- He could select all the government ministers.
- He and the cabinet would propose laws to the Reichstag.
- He was responsible for law and order, taxation, schooling, health care etc.
- He had to have the support of the majority of the Reichstag to bring in new laws.
- He could be dismissed by the president.

## What was the role of the Reichstag in the Weimar Republic?

The Reichstag had many powers but they were limited:

- The Reichstag had more power than the Reichsrat.
- It controlled taxation.
- There had to be elections to the Reichstag at least every 4 years.
- It had the power to create laws but the Reichsrat had to agree to them.

## What was the role of the Reichsrat in the Weimar Republic?

The Reichsrat had some powers but the powers were limited:

- The Reichsrat had to be elected every 4 years.
- It could advise the Reichstag on the new laws, but the Reichstag could overrule it.
- It represented all those regions of Weimar Germany that elected representatives.

## What was Article 48 of the Weimar Republic?

The constitution of the Weimar Republic included Article 48. This allowed the chancellor to ask the president to take emergency measures without the support of the Reichstag.

## What were the Weimar Republic's constitutional strengths?

There were 5 key strengths of the new constitution which prevented any one person or group gaining too much power:

- All Germans aged 21 and over, men and women, were allowed to vote so it was very democratic.

- ☑ The Reichstag was elected using proportional representation which meant a party was given a certain number of seats according to how many votes it gained in the election. This was considered fairer for smaller parties.
- ☑ The constitution was written in such a way that the power of one person or institution would be limited and therefore, they would not have too much power.
- ☑ The chancellor introduced new laws, but they only became laws if the majority of the Reichstag and Reichsrat voted for them.
- ☑ The Reichstag had more power but the Reichsrat could delay passing laws.

### What were the weaknesses of the Weimar Republic's constitution?

There were 4 principal weaknesses of the Weimar Republic's constitution:

- ☑ Proportional representation often meant no single party won enough seats to form a government on its own, so several parties had to form a coalition governments which often fell apart.
- ☑ Article 48 of the constitution gave the president the power to take emergency measures, by-passing the Reichstag. This could effectively create another dictatorship, in all but name.
- ☑ Many judges and civil servants did not want the Weimar Republic and so did not fully support it.
- ☑ The leaders of the army wanted the kaiser back and did not support the Weimar Republic.

### What happened when the Weimar Republic stopped paying reparations?

The Weimar Republic paid reparations after the First World War but then defaulted at the end of 1922. France and Belgium took action in January 1923 by occupying the Ruhr to collect the money owed. This led to hyperinflation.

### What was the political system of the Weimar Republic?

There were 5 key reasons why politics in the Weimar Republic were difficult:

- ☑ The electoral system used proportional representation which meant that the number of seats a political party gained was in proportion to the number of votes cast for them in the election.
- ☑ Therefore, there were many different parties that could be elected to the Reichstag.
- ☑ Coalition governments were formed of more than one party. For example, in 1925 the government was made up of 5 different political parties.
- ☑ This made politics difficult because the parties had different beliefs and would rarely agree.
- ☑ During the crisis of the Great Depression, a number of coalition governments regularly collapsed.

### What was the political makeup of parties in the Weimar Republic?

There were more than 29 political parties across the political spectrum throughout the Weimar period.

### Which political parties were the most important of the Weimar Republic?

The 5 most important parties were:

- ☑ The Communists (KPD); an extreme left-wing party.
- ☑ The Social Democrats (SPD); moderately left-wing.
- ☑ The Centre Party (ZP); in the middle.
- ☑ The German People's Party (DVP); moderately right-wing.
- ☑ The Nationalist Socialist Party (NSDAP *(p.44)*) ; the Nazi Party and extremely right-wing.

### What was the Communist Party in the Weimar Republic?

The Communist Party, or KPD, of the Weimar Republic was:

- ☑ An extreme left-wing party that believed in communism and revolution.
- ☑ Opposed the Weimar Republic and wanted it to fail.

- Supported by the working class and some middle class people.
- Supported by the Spartacists who led the Spartacist Revolt (p.27) in 1919 which tried to overthrow the Weimar Republic.
- Well funded by the USSR.

## What was the Social Democratic Party in the Weimar Republic?

The Social Democratic Party, or SPD, of the Weimar Republic was:

- Moderately left-wing.
- Supported by the working class and the middle class.
- Anti-communist.
- Very supportive of the Weimar Republic that they helped to create.
- President Ebert's party.

## What was the Centre Party in the Weimar Republic?

The Centre Party, or ZP, of the Weimar Republic was:

- A moderate political party.
- Supported by conservatives and Catholics as it used to be the party of the Catholic Church.
- Supported the Weimar Republic.
- A part of every coalition government from 1919 to 1933.

## What was the German People's Party in the Weimar Republic?

The German People's Party, or DVP, was:

- A moderate political party.
- Supported by the upper middle classes.
- Mostly supportive of the Weimar Republic but they had concerns.
- Tended to support the monarchy.
- The party of Stresemann, the Chancellor in 1923 and Foreign Secretary between 1923 and 1929.

## What was the Nazi Party in the Weimar Republic?

The Nationalist Socialist Party, NSDAP (p.44), or Nazi Party was:

- Extremely right-wing and nationalistic.
- Strongly opposed the Weimar Republic and wanted to overthrow it.
- Supported by the wealthy, businessmen, ex-soldiers, workers and the middle classes.
- Led by Adolf Hitler (p.102).
- Anti-communist.

---

**DID YOU KNOW?**

**The announcement of a German Republic was accidental.**

Philipp Scheidemann announced that Germany was a republic from the balcony of the Reichstag to prevent a communist state from being set up. This seriously angered Ebert, who was a monarchist.

# TREATY OF VERSAILLES, 1919

*The Treaty of Versailles ended the First World War but it horrified Germans who called it the 'Diktat' or dictated peace.*

### What was the Treaty of Versailles?
The Treaty of Versailles was the peace document which officially ended the First World War between Germany and the Allied Powers.

### When was the Treaty of Versailles signed?
The Treaty of Versailles was signed on 28th June, 1919.

### Where was the Treaty of Versailles signed?
The treaty was signed in the Hall of Mirrors in the Palace of Versailles, France.

### What were the terms of the Treaty of Versailles?
There were various terms Germany had to agree to, including taking the blame for the First World War, military reductions, territorial losses and financial payments (reparations) to the Allies.

### What were the military terms of the Treaty of Versailles?
There were 8 key military restrictions to which Germany agreed:
- Limiting its army to 100,000 men.
- Limiting its navy to 15,000 men, 6 battleships and no submarines.
- The Rhineland was demilitarised which meant no German armed forces were allowed to enter.
- No military air force was allowed.
- Conscription was banned so all soldiers had to be volunteers.
- No tanks or armoured cars were allowed.
- No heavy artillery was allowed.
- The Allies would station an army of occupation on the west bank of the Rhine in the towns of Cologne, Coblenz and Mainz.

### What were the financial terms of the Treaty of Versailles?
There were 3 key financial restrictions to which Germany agreed:
- Germany was forced to pay reparations, or compensation, to the Allies for the destruction of land and the death of soldiers in the First World War.
- The debt that Germany owed was set at £6.6 billion in 1921.
- Germany had to give up its merchant fleet to Britain as compensation for the ships it had sunk during the war.

### What was the 'war guilt clause' of the Treaty of Versailles?
Article 231 was the 'war guilt clause' that forced Germany to accept the blame for causing the war. This enabled the Allies to demand reparations or compensation from Germany.

### What were the territorial terms of the Treaty of Versailles?
There were 11 main territorial adjustments:
- Alsace-Lorraine was returned from Germany to France.
- Eupen-Malmedy was taken from Germany and given to Belgium.

- They lost Posen and West Prussia to Poland, which resulted in Germany being divided in two. East Prussia was cut off from the rest of Germany by an area of land called the Polish Corridor.
- The German port of Danzig was made an international city, under the control of the League of Nations, which meant it was not ruled by Germany. Danzig was used by Poland as a port.
- Germany lost all 11 colonies. They were handed over to the League of Nations who gave them as mandates to victorious countries, including Britain, France and Japan.
- Two areas of Germany were given a public vote, or plebiscite, to decide whether they would belong to Germany or not. Upper Silesia voted to join Poland. North Schleswig voted to join Denmark.
- France would be given the coal output of the Saar coal mines for 15 years and the Saar would be administered by the League of Nations.
- Germany lost 13% of its land in Europe and 10% of its population.
- The Treaty of Brest-Litovsk was cancelled. Estonia, Latvia and Lithuania were taken from Germany and turned into independent states.
- Memel was given to Lithuania. Hultschin was given to Czechoslovakia.
- Germany was also prohibited from the Anschluss, which meant it could not unite with Austria.

## What was the German reaction to the Treaty of Versailles?

Germany reacted in 6 key ways:

- The majority of Germans were angered by the treaty and highly resented several of its terms.
- Germans were given no say in the treaty. They saw it as a diktat, or a dictated peace.
- The new Weimar government earned itself the nickname the November Criminals because Germans believed they had been betrayed by their government when it signed the Treaty of Versailles.
- Some Germans thought the war guilt clause (Article 231) was unfair and it wasn't right to blame the new Weimar government for the actions of the now-abdicated kaiser.
- The restriction of the armed forces hurt Germany's pride and made it feel weak, particularly next to its armed neighbours.
- Germany felt further insulted by not being allowed to join the League of Nations until it had proven itself a peaceful nation.

> **DID YOU KNOW?**
>
> **Initially, the representative of Germany refused to sign the Treaty of Versailles.**
>
> The Allies had to threatened to end the cease-fire and re-start the war, for Germany to sign the Treaty.

# WHAT ARE LEFT-WING VIEWS?

*The left-wing views of the socialists and the communists.*

## What are left-wing views?

Political parties that are described as 'left-wing' want to change society so that it becomes fairer and there is greater equality between the classes. They want governments to rule for the benefit of the working class. Left-wing views can be divided into moderate with socialist views or extreme left-wing with communist views.

### What are the views of moderate left-wing parties?

There are 4 main beliefs that moderate left-wing or socialist parties hold:

- Economically, they would prefer a country in which large businesses are owned by the state and wealth is redistributed from the rich to the poor through taxation.
- Socially, they want greater equality between the rich and poor so that the gap between them in terms of wealth is narrowed.
- They want more political power in the hands of the workers.
- They believe in international cooperation.

### What are the views of extreme left-wing parties?

There are 4 main beliefs that extreme left-wing or communist parties hold:

- Economically, they want to abolish private ownership of property, business and land. Instead, the state or government would own them on behalf of the working class.
- They want political power to be in the hands of the working class, often in the form of a dictatorship.
- They want to completely change society so there is no gap between the rich and poor, to achieve equality for all.
- They believe that the whole world should undergo these changes, a worldwide communist revolution.

> **DID YOU KNOW?**
>
> **The phrase 'left-wing' came from the French Revolution.**
> As the new constitution was debated, the anti-royalist revolutionaries were on the left-hand side of the Assembly Hall.

## WHAT ARE RIGHT-WING VIEWS?

*The right-wing views of the conservatives and fascists.*

### What are right-wing views?

Political parties that are described as 'right-wing' often do not want change as they believe in traditional values. They favour capitalism so accept a greater divide between the rich and the poor. Right-wing views can be divided into moderate conservative views or extreme right-wing with fascist views.

### What are the views of moderate right-wing parties?

There are 4 main beliefs that moderate right-wing or conservative political parties hold:

- Economically, they believe in capitalism and the private ownership of property, business and land. Taxes should be low.
- They tend to want political power to be in the hands of the upper classes.
- They want to keep society as it is and do not favour rapid change. They believe in more traditional family values and law and order.
- They believe in international competition in terms of trade and that their nation takes priority over others.

### What are the views of extreme right-wing parties?

There are 5 main beliefs that extreme right-wing or fascist parties hold:

- Economically, they favour private ownership of business, property and land. However, the economy should be controlled to benefit the nation to make it strong.
- Politically, they want a strong centralised or authoritarian government often with one leader in the form of a dictator.
- Socially, they prefer traditional family values and law and order. They restrict people's freedoms and rights.
- The interests of the nation are greater than those of the individual.
- They are very nationalistic and often want to expand how much territory their country controls.

> **DID YOU KNOW?**
>
> **The phrase 'right-wing' came from the French Revolution.**
> The pro-royalist supporters were on the right-hand side of the Assembly Hall as they debated a new constitution.

# POLITICAL CHALLENGES

*The new Weimar Republic faced enormous challenges in its early years.*

## What early political challenges did the Weimar Republic face?

There were political challenges to the Weimar Republic *(p.18)* from the left and the right in the early years.

## When did the Weimar Republic face political challenges initially?

It faced political challenges between 1919 and 1923.

## Why did the Weimar Republic face political challenges in the early years?

There were 4 key reasons why there were political challenges:

- Signing the Treaty of Versailles made the Weimar Republic *(p.18)* unpopular.
- The belief that the Weimar politicians had 'stabbed Germany in the back' and were 'November criminals' for signing the armistice and the Treaty of Versailles became popular opinion.
- Extreme left-wing parties wanted a communist government in Germany. They wanted to end capitalism - this meant that they wanted to end private ownership of land, business and property. They wanted workers to have power.
- Extreme right-wing parties wanted a very strong government with a strong army. Some wanted the kaiser back. They hated the Weimar Republic *(p.18)* because they saw it as weak.

> **DID YOU KNOW?**
>
> **The Treaty of Versailles was a cause of the hatred for the Weimar Republic.**
> Germans believed the Weimar politicians had 'stabbed them in the back' by signing the treaty.

# POLITICAL VIOLENCE

*The early years of the Weimar Republic were fraught with political assassinations.*

### What political violence did the Weimar Republic face in the early years?
During the early years the Weimar Republic *(p.18)* faced a lot of political violence. Many people were murdered, including politicians.

### When did the political violence occur in the Weimar Republic?
The political violence occurred between 1919 and 1923.

### Why was there political violence in the Weimar Republic?
It happened because of the Weimar Republic's *(p.18)* unpopularity with certain left-wing and right-wing groups, which resulted in uprisings and political assassinations.

### How many were targeted by the political violence in the Weimar Republic?
Between 1919 and 1922 there were 376 political murders.

### Who was targeted by the political violence in the Weimar Republic?
There were three notable ones:
- In 1919, a member of the Council of People's Representatives, Hugo Haase, was assassinated.
- In August 1921, Matthias Erzberger was assassinated because he was viewed as a November Criminal for signing the armistice in November 1918.
- In June 1922, the Weimar Republic's *(p.18)* foreign minister, Walther Rathenau, was assassinated.

### How did the Weimar Republic deal with the political violence?
Those accused of committing the murders were treated differently. The judges were harsher on those who were left-wing, with ten left-wing assassins convicted and executed. Nobody accused of murder who was right-wing was convicted.

### What role did the political parties play in the political violence in the Weimar Republic?
Political violence was made worse by the political parties because they had their own private armies or paramilitary forces. The KPD had the Red Front Fighters, for example, while the DNVP had the Stahlhelm.

### What was the importance of the political violence in the Weimar Republic?
The political violence was important because it showed that the Weimar Republic *(p.18)* was so unpopular with some political groups that they were prepared to break the law in an attempt to achieve what they wanted.

---

**DID YOU KNOW?**

**There were more political assassinations committed by people with right-wing views than left-wing.**

Of the 376 political murders between 1919 and 1922, 354 were committed by people with right-wing views. None of right-wing murderers were executed, but 10 left-wing murderers were.

# SPARTACIST REVOLT, 1919

*The Spartacists were named after a slave, Spartacus, who led a rebellion against the Romans.*

### What was the Spartacist Revolt?

The Spartacist Revolt, or Spartacist uprising, was an attempted revolution to overthrow the Weimar Republic (p.18) by an extreme left-wing group called the Spartacists.

### When was the Spartacist Revolt?

The Spartacist Revolt took place between 5th and 12th January, 1919.

### Who led the Spartacist Revolt?

The Spartacists were an extreme left-wing group that supported the German Communist Party. They were extreme socialists from the Independent Socialist Party (USPD). They were led by Rosa Luxemburg and Karl Liebknecht.

### Where was the Spartacist Revolt?

The Spartacist Revolt took place in Berlin.

### Why did the Spartacist Revolt occur?

There were 3 key reasons why the Spartacist Revolt occurred:

- It took place because Chancellor Ebert sacked the chief of police of Berlin, Emil Eichhorn, on 4th January, 1919. The workers supported Eichhorn so there were protests.
- The Spartacists used this as an opportunity to stage an uprising on 5th January.
- They wanted Germany to be run by small councils of soldiers and workers similar to what was set up in Russia in the February Revolution of 1917.

### What were the key events of the Spartacist Revolt?

There were 7 main events of the Spartacist Uprising:

- The party launched a bid for power on the 5th of January 1919, led by both Liebknecht and Luxemburg.
- They were soon joined by resentful soldiers and sailors and there was a mass demonstration of 100,000 other workers.
- The Spartacists took over key buildings, including the newspaper and telegraph offices, and the government lost control.
- However, some anti-communist soldiers formed another group called the Freikorps who were not supportive of the Spartacists.
- Ebert made an agreement with the Freikorps, so long as they crushed the Spartacists along with the help of the army.
- The two sides fought on the streets, and there were resulting high losses. The Freikorps were victorious, and Luxemburg and Liebknecht were murdered.
- The Spartacist uprising had failed, however other revolutions soon followed.

### How did the Weimar Republic react to the Spartacist Revolt?

The government reacted in 3 main ways:

- The government needed military support. However, the German Army, the Reichswehr, was too weak, so Ebert ordered it to use the Freikorps, ex-soldiers who had kept their weapons from the First World War.
- The Freikorps were used by the government to crush the Spartacist Revolt. By March 1919, there were approximately 250,000 members of the Freikorps. They were very right-wing and hated the communists.

- The Freikorps arrested and brutally murdered Karl Liebknecht and Rosa Luxemburg on 16th January, 1919. Several thousand communist supporters were arrested and killed during the uprising.

### Why was the Spartacist Revolt important?
The Spartacist uprising was important for 3 key reasons:
- It showed that the Weimar Republic *(p.18)* was weak and unpopular.
- It gave the Freikorps a lot of power as they were allowed by the government to attack and kill the Spartacists without being arrested themselves.
- The Weimar Republic *(p.18)* survived and the German Army had supported it when it was needed.

> **DID YOU KNOW?**
> The Spartacists were brutally crushed by the Freikorps.
> There are memorials to Rosa Luxemburg and Karl Liebknecht in Berlin, as well as streets and squares named after them.

# THE KAPP PUTSCH, 1920
*The Kapp Putsch highlighted the tensions between the Republic and the army.*

### What was the Kapp Putsch?
The Kapp Putsch was a right-wing uprising against the Weimar Republic *(p.18)*.

### When was the Kapp Putsch?
The Kapp Putsch happened in March 1920.

### Where was the Kapp Putsch?
The Kapp Putsch happened in Berlin.

### Who was involved in the Kapp Putsch?
It was organised by the Freikorps (ex-soldiers) and led by Dr Wolfgang Kapp.

### Why did the Kapp Putsch occur?
There are 4 key reasons why the Kapp Putsch took place:
- A group of anti-communist ex-soldiers called the Freikorps had grown by 1920 and President Ebert could not control them. In March 1920, the Weimar government announced the Freikorps would be disbanded.
- The leaders of the putsch wanted to take over the country, make the army strong again and then recover the lands Germany had lost in the Treaty of Versailles. They wanted their empire once again.
- They deeply resented the Treaty of Versailles for their crippled economy.
- Some wanted the kaiser to return from exile.

### What were the key events of the Kapp Putsch?
There were 4 key events:

- The Freikorps reacted to the government's disbanding of the group by marching into Berlin with around 5,000 men.
- Members of the army refused to fire on them as they were ex-soldiers.
- The rebels took control of Berlin and they looked to be successful. However, the government was saved by the industrial workers of Berlin who went on strike - as a result the capital came to a halt.
- With no power, water or resources, it became clear to Dr Kapp that they could not succeed. He fled the country and later died before coming to trial.

### How did the Weimar Republic react to the Kapp Putsch?

The Weimar Republic *(p.18)* took 4 key actions:

- The government fled to Dresden as Berlin was under the control of the rebels.
- They asked the public to go on strike which stopped gas, electricity, water and transport services.
- The rebels fled after realising they could not govern the country.
- Kapp was captured in April 1922 when he returned to Germany from Sweden, but died while waiting to be put on trial.

### Why was the Kapp Putsch important to the Weimar Republic?

The Kapp Putsch was important because it showed how unpopular the Weimar Republic *(p.18)* was with right-wing parties, and that the army would not support it if the extreme right launched an attack.

> **DID YOU KNOW?**
>
> **3 facts about Dr Wolfgang Kapp:**
> - He was born in America.
> - He was very nationalistic.
> - The rebels declared him to be the chancellor during the putsch.

# THE RUHR CRISIS, 1923

*The occupation of the Ruhr in 1923 by French and Belgian troops, led to the major economic crisis of hyperinflation.*

### What was the Ruhr Occupation?

The Ruhr Occupation was a period of military occupation by France and Belgium of the Ruhr region in Germany. It happened because Germany failed to pay the reparations instalment at the end of 1922.

### When was the Ruhr Occupation?

The Ruhr Occupation took place between 11th January, 1923 and 25th August, 1925.

### Which countries were involved with the Ruhr Occupation?

France and Belgium were the occupying countries.

### Why did the Ruhr Occupation occur?

The Ruhr Occupation occurred because of 4 main reasons:

- By the end of 1922, Germany stated that they would miss the next reparation payment that was due.

- In response, the French and Belgians took control of the area because it was Germany's main industrial area.
- They were then able to take goods or resources from the Ruhr as a form of reparations.
- The terms of the Treaty of Versailles meant this was legal.

### What actions did France and Belgium take during the Ruhr Occupation?

France and Belgium took 6 main actions:

- Sent in 60,000 French and Belgian soldiers.
- Took over factories, mines and railways.
- Took food and goods.
- Arrested Germans and 100 Germans were killed.
- Threw 15,000 Germans out of their homes.
- They forced over 100,000 protesters to leave the area.

### What was Germany's response to the Ruhr Occupation?

Germany responded in 4 main ways:

- The German government ordered its workers in the Ruhr to not fight back.
- Instead, the German workers used passive resistance. They went on strike. They would not help the French or Belgium troops remove coal or manufactured goods from the Ruhr.
- France and Belgium brought in their own workers to take their place.
- The government's halting of production of the largest industrial region in Germany, crippled the country's economy.

### What were the consequences of the Ruhr Occupation?

There were 4 important consequences of the Ruhr Occupation:

- The Weimar Republic *(p.18)* responded by printing more money to pay the reparations bill and the striking Ruhr workers.
- Printing money led to hyperinflation where money became worthless and the price of goods drastically increased. For example, the price of bread in the summer of 1923 was 1,200 marks but by November 1923 it was 428 billion marks!
- It was one of the causes of the Nazi *(p.44)* Munich Beer Hall Putsch *(p.46)*, 1923.
- The Dawes Plan *(p.32)*, 1924 brought about the end of the hyperinflation problem and Ruhr occupation.

---

**DID YOU KNOW?**

**The crises of 1923 encouraged Hitler to organise his Beer Hall Putsch.**

He thought it was a perfect opportunity as there was so much discontent in Weimar Germany at that time.

# HYPERINFLATION, 1923

*Hyperinflation severely tested the Weimar Republic and brought great hardship to many.*

## What caused the hyperinflation crisis in Weimar Republic?

To pay reparations and the workers striking in the Ruhr, Germany printed more money. This led to hyperinflation and had a disastrous effect on the economy. The value of the German mark fell and the prices of goods increased.

## What were the economic consequences of the hyperinflation crisis in the Weimar Republic?

There were 7 main economic consequences of hyperinflation.

- With prices rising by the hour, people began to buy goods as soon as they were paid. A loaf of bread in 1922 cost 200 marks. By 1923 it cost 200,000 million marks.
- Many people used a barter system and traded items instead of paying with money to get around the problems of hyperinflation.
- As money became worthless, those with savings lost their money. This especially affected the middle classes.
- People used the money in other ways, such as burning it for fuel. Children would also play with it, while some even made dresses from it!
- People on fixed incomes could not renegotiate their earnings and the elderly on fixed pensions received no increases. This meant their incomes became almost worthless.
- Many small business owners went bankrupt.
- Foreign businesses would not accept the worthless currency which led to shortages of imported goods.

## Who benefitted from the hyperinflation crisis in the Weimar Republic?

There were 3 main benefits of hyperinflation:

- Those with debts found it easier to pay off what they owed.
- Farmers benefitted from the increase in food prices because people were paying more for food.
- Foreign visitors benefitted. They could buy more with their money because they could exchange their currency for more German marks. This made the people very angry.

## What was the solution to the hyperinflation crisis in the Weimar Republic?

The hyperinflation crisis was solved in 3 key ways:

- Stresemann, as chancellor, replaced the worthless currency with a temporary one called the Rentenmark in October 1924.
- Eventually the Rentenmark became the new Reichsmark in 1924. This was a stable currency that remained for the next 25 years.
- Stresemann, as foreign secretary, signed the Dawes Plan *(p.32)* in 1924 which organised American loans to German banks and businesses and temporarily lowered annual reparation payments to help the German economy recover.

## How successful was the solution to the hyperinflation crisis?

Stresemann's solution to the hyperinflation crisis had 2 main successes:

- People accepted the new currency and hyperinflation ended.
- The Dawes Plan *(p.32)*, 1924 helped to restore economic stability.

## How did the solution to hyperinflation fall short?

Stresemann's solution to the hyperinflation crisis had 3 main failures:

- People who lost savings, mainly the middle classes, never received their money back and they blamed the Weimar Republic *(p.18)* for this.

- People who had suffered during the hyperinflation crisis were bitter about their experience and blamed the Weimar Republic *(p.18)*.
- One of the reasons the Nazi Party *(p.44)* organised the Munich Beer Hall Putsch *(p.46)* in 1923 was because of the hyperinflation crisis.

> **DID YOU KNOW?**
>
> **A historian offered this anecdote from 1923 to highlight the effects of hyperinflation:**
>
> 'Two women were carrying a laundry basket filled to the brim with banknotes. ...they put down the basket, ...... When they turned round a few moments later, they found the money there untouched. But the basket was gone'.

# DAWES PLAN, 1924

*The Dawes Plan rescued the German economy and enabled Germany to recover.*

### What was the Dawes Plan?
The Dawes Plan was an agreement between the USA and Weimar Germany which helped to solve Germany's problems in paying reparations.

### When was the Dawes Plan signed?
The Dawes Plan was negotiated in April 1924 and signed in October 1924.

### Who created the Dawes Plan?
The Dawes Plan was created by American banker, Charles G Dawes *(p.96)*, along with Gustav Stresemann *(p.109)*.

### Why was the Dawes Plan created?
The Dawes Plan was created to solve Germany's problems in paying reparations following the 1923 hyperinflation crisis.

### What was agreed in the Dawes Plan?
The Dawes Plan included 3 key terms:
- A temporary reduction in the annual reparations repayments to £50 million.
- US banks and businesses offered loans worth 800 million marks to German industries and businesses.
- The German State Bank, the Reichsbank, should be reorganised and supervised by the Allies.

### What were the benefits of the Dawes Plan?
There were 3 main benefits of the Dawes Plan:
- American loans helped industrial output to double between 1923 and 1928. Employment, income tax and trade all increased as a result.
- The French and Belgians left the Ruhr as they were promised that they would receive reparations as result of the Dawes Plan.
- The Weimar Republic *(p.18)* became politically stronger as the economy improved.

## What were the criticisms of the Dawes Plan?

There were 2 key criticisms of the Dawes Plan:

- In the short-term, both the extreme left-wing and extreme right-wing political parties were angry Germany was still paying reparations imposed by the Treaty of Versailles.
- In the long term, because the Weimar economy was dependent on US loans, Germany could be economically damaged if these were suddenly recalled.

> **DID YOU KNOW?**
>
> The Dawes Plan saved the Weimar Republic in the short term with American loans. However, in the long term, when the American economy crashed in 1929, so too did Germany's.

# LOCARNO PACT, 1925
*The Locarno Pact protected Franco-German and Belgo-German borders.*

## What was the Locarno Pact?

The Locarno Pact was a treaty intended to improve the relationship between Germany, Belgium and France by protecting their borders.

## When was the Locarno Pact signed?

The Locarno Pact was signed in December 1925.

## Who signed the Locarno Pact?

The pact was signed by Germany, Belgium, France, Britain and Italy.

## Why was the Locarno Pact signed?

It was intended to improve the relationship between Germany and her neighbours. German leader, Gustav Stresemann *(p.109)*, also wanted to prevent them from being invaded again after the French and Belgian occupation of the Ruhr *(p.29)* in 1923.

## What were the terms of the Locarno Pact?

There were 5 key terms of the Locarno Pact:

- Germany accepted its new borders with France, drawn up under the Treaty of Versailles. France pledged peace with Germany; it would not occupy Germany again.
- Germany accepted its new borders with Belgium, drawn up under the Treaty of Versailles, and Belgium pledged peace with Germany.
- If there was a border dispute between Germany and France or Germany and Belgium, Britain and Italy would step in as guarantors to solve the problems.
- The five countries agreed to discuss Germany's membership of the League of Nations.
- It was agreed the Rhineland would be permanently demilitarised.

### What were the benefits of the Locarno Pact?

There were 4 key benefits of the Locarno Pact:

- War was less likely because the relationships between Germany, France, Britain, Belgium and Italy improved.
- Germany was treated like an equal, rather than the loser of the First World War.
- As the Locarno Pact had been negotiated between Germany and the other countries, unlike the Treaty of Versailles, it was more acceptable to the public. It improved the reputation of the government and increased support for the moderate political parties.
- It paved the way for Germany to join the League of Nations.

### What were the criticisms of the Locarno Pact?

The drawback of the Locarno Pact was that extremist political parties hated it, primarily because it confirmed the borders laid out in the detested Treaty of Versailles.

> **DID YOU KNOW?**
>
> **The Locarno Pact symbolised part of a period called the 'Locarno Era' or 'Locarno honeymoon.'**
>
> The Locarno Era was during the 1920s and seemed to promise a period of reconciliation - after horrors of the First World War - that was tied to the hopes for disarmament.

## LEAGUE OF NATIONS, 1926

*Signing the Locarno Pact in 1925 opened the door to Germany's entry to the League of Nations in 1926.*

### What made Weimar Germany join the League of Nations?

Following successful discussions at the Locarno Conference, Weimar Germany joined the League of Nations.

### When did Weimar Germany join the League of Nations?

Weimar Germany joined the League of Nations in September 1926.

### How did being able to join the League of Nations benefit Weimar Germany?

There were 3 main benefits of joining the League of Nations:

- It helped improve confidence in the government and restore national pride.
- Germany was now accepted as a member of the international community once more.
- Weimar Germany was given a place on the League of Nations Council, which took the most important decisions in the League.

### How did being able to join the League of Nations affect Weimar Germany negatively?

The negative results were that some parties in the Weimar Republic *(p. 18)* strongly disagreed with membership of the League of Nations. They saw the League as a symbol of the hated Treaty of Versailles, as the treaty had helped to establish the League.

> **DID YOU KNOW?**
> Germany was a part of the League of Nations permanent council.

# KELLOGG-BRIAND PACT, 1928

*The Kellogg-Briand Pact was not enforceable if a signatory used war as a means of achieving their foreign policy aims.*

### What was the Kellogg-Briand Pact?

The Kellogg-Briand Pact was a promise by countries who signed it not to use war to achieve their foreign policy aims.

### When was the Kellogg-Briand Pact signed?

The Kellogg-Briand Pact was signed in August 1928.

### Who signed the Kellogg-Briand Pact?

The Kellogg-Briand pact was an agreement between 62 nations, including Germany. It was organised by the US foreign minister, Kellogg, and the French foreign minister, Briand.

### What were the benefits for Germany of signing the Kellogg-Briand Pact?

There were 3 main benefits of the Kellogg-Briand Pact:

- ✅ It showed that moderate political parties could build Germany's international strength and standing.
- ✅ It improved the reputation of the Weimar Republic *(p.18)*.
- ✅ Germany was now being included as one of the world's main powers.

### Was there any negative reaction to the Kellogg-Briand Pact?

There were also some negative reactions. For example, not all Germans supported the Kellogg-Briand Pact because it didn't remove the restrictions placed on Germany by the Treaty of Versailles.

> **DID YOU KNOW?**
>
> **3 facts about Frank B Kellogg:**
> - ✓ He studied law.
> - ✓ He was awarded the Nobel Peace Prize in 1929 because of the Kellogg-Briand Pact.
> - ✓ He was a member of the Permanent Court of International Justice.

# YOUNG PLAN, 1929

*Hitler said the Young Plan extending reparation payments over 59 years was 'passing the penalty onto the unborn.'*

### What was the Young Plan?
The Young Plan was another deal that aimed to help Germany pay the reparations bill.

### When was the Young Plan created?
The Young Plan was signed in August 1929.

### Who created the Young Plan?
Owen Young *(p.111)*, an American banker, helped negotiate the Young Plan with Stresemann and Germany.

### Why was the Young Plan needed?
The Young Plan was created to help Weimar Germany pay its reparations bill.

### What was agreed in the Young Plan?
The Young Plan stated Germany would have 59 years to pay the reparations bill, which was reduced from £6.6 billion to £2 billion.

### What were the benefits of the Young Plan?
There were 3 key benefits of the Young Plan:
- The lower reparations payments meant the Weimar government could in turn reduce taxes, giving people more money to spend or save.
- It helped them recover economically.
- It increased confidence politically.

### How did the Young Plan not help Weimar Germany?
There were 2 key criticisms of the Young Plan:
- The reparations payment was still high at £50 million per year.
- The extreme political parties were furious that reparations had not been cancelled. Hitler commented that extending payments over 59 years was "passing the penalty onto the unborn.".

---

**DID YOU KNOW?**

**3 facts about the Young Plan:**
- ✓ J P Morgan was a member of the committee that drew up the Young Plan.
- ✓ The Young Plan was abandoned in 1932 because of the Wall Street Crash and subsequent Great Depression.
- ✓ The DNVP and the NSDAP both campaigned against the Young Plan.

# FULLY RECOVERED?

*Historians still debate to what extent Weimar Germany recovered between 1924 and 1929.*

### Did the Weimar Republic recover between 1924 and 1929?

There is some debate about how far the Weimar Republic *(p.18)* recovered between 1924 and 1929, following the hyperinflation crisis. There is evidence to suggest the Republic did recover but not fully.

### What evidence is there to suggest that the Weimar Republic did recover between 1924 and 1929?

There are 9 main pieces of evidence to suggest that the Weimar Republic *(p.18)* did recover:

- The temporary currency, the Rentenmark, replaced the worthless German Mark and gradually restored confidence.
- There was greater political stability. The moderate Social Democrats Party won the most votes in general elections. There was greater backing for the political parties that supported the Weimar Republic *(p.18)*.
- Support for the extreme political parties decreased as support for the moderate parties increased. The Nazi Party *(p.44)* only won 12 seats in the May 1928 elections.
- The German economy improved with the loans from the US. Businesses were able to pay off their debts and industrial production grew between 1923 and 1929.
- Gustav Stresemann *(p.109)* was greatly praised for his policies and many felt the recovery was due to his leadership.
- The wages of industrial workers increased slightly and there were fewer strikes, suggesting workers were happier.
- By 1928, industrial production had recovered and reached pre-war levels.
- By 1930, Germany was one of leading exporters of manufactured goods.
- Greater economic prosperity led to an explosion of culture. This became known as the "Golden Age".

### What evidence is there to suggest that the Weimar Republic did not fully recover between 1924 and 1929?

There are 7 main pieces of evidence to suggest that the Weimar Republic *(p.18)* did not fully recover:

- Extremist parties such as the communists and Nazis *(p.44)* that wanted to destroy the Weimar Republic *(p.18)* still existed and had supporters.
- Germany was dependent on its loans from the US. If America recalled the loans, the German economy would suffer.
- Although unemployment *(p.83)* did fall between between 1924 and 1929, it never went below 1.3 million.
- Agriculture did not thrive and farmers struggled. They made little profit and fell into greater debt. They did not have the money to invest in new machinery to modernise their practices. Production was still lower than before the First World War.
- The basic problem of the constitution remained. As the election system used proportional representation, no one party could secure a majority in the Reichstag and as a result there were frequent, short-lived coalition governments.
- The cost of living rose and the increase in wages was mostly wiped out by higher prices.
- Many nationalists opposed the Dawes and Young *(p.80)* plans because the plans meant that Weimar Germany still had to accept the terms of the Treaty of Versailles.

---

**DID YOU KNOW?**

**3 facts about Gustav Stresemann:**
- ✓ He served as chancellor for a total of 102 days.
- ✓ He was a member of the German Democratic Party from 1918-1929.
- ✓ He won the Nobel Peace Prize in 1926.

# STANDARD OF LIVING IN WEIMAR GERMANY

*Life in Weimar Germany improved in many ways.*

### What was the standard of living in Weimar Germany like?

For most people, there was some improvements in the standard of living between 1924 and 1929 in Weimar Germany. However, there were still issues.

### How did unemployment insurance affect the standard of living in Weimar Germany?

The standard of living between 1924 and 1929 was affected by the introduction of the Unemployment *(p.83)* Insurance Act in 1927. This meant that workers paid a small amount of their wages into the insurance scheme. If they were made unemployed or fell sick they received 60 marks per week.

### How did work and wages affect the standard of living in Weimar Germany?

The standard of living between 1924 and 1929 was affected by an increase in wages between 1925 and 1928. Wages increased by 25% in real terms which meant that the wage increase was above the rate of inflation.

### How did housing affect the standard of living in Weimar Germany?

The standard of living between 1924 and 1929 was affected by improvements in housing. There was a shortage in houses. The government dealt with the problem in several ways, for example by introducing tax breaks and government spending. By 1928, more houses were built but there was still a shortage.

### What other improvements affected the standard of living in Weimar Germany?

The standard of living between 1924 and 1929 was affected by other government measures such as pensions being paid to war veterans and war widows with the introduction of the Reich Pension Law of 1920, and the government reformed the system protecting the youth *(p.80)* by introducing more social workers.

### How did the standard of living change in Weimar Germany?

Overall, the standard of living between 1924 and 1929 did improve in terms of housing, wages and unemployment *(p.83)* insurance. However, the recovery was not secure as people were still suffering from the effects of the hyperinflation crisis of 1923.

> **DID YOU KNOW?**
>
> The improvements in the standard of living and the economy were very much based on the loans from America organised through the Dawes Plan of 1924.

# SOCIAL CHANGES FOR WOMEN

*Women in Weimar Germany experienced increased rights but they still faced sexism and inequality in the workplace.*

### What happened to the lives of women in the Weimar Republic?

Between 1924 and 1929, women in the Weimar Republic *(p.18)* enjoyed more social, political and economic freedom but there were limitations.

### What happened to a woman's life politically in the Weimar Republic?

There were 3 main political changes to the lives of women in the Weimar Republic *(p.18)*:

- Women aged 21 years and over were given the right to vote.
- There were 112 female members of the Reichstag by 1932.
- The constitution gave women and men equal rights. Women gained more political rights.

### What happened to a woman's life economically in the Weimar Republic?

Women's lives did not change that much in terms of economics and work:

- In 1918, 75% of women were working - mainly because of the First World War - but this figure dropped to 36% by 1925.
- Despite gaining political equality with men in the constitution, women were paid less than men.
- Women found it difficult to have a professional career. There were few female judges but women were more successful in medicine and education.

### What happened to women's lives socially in the Weimar Republic?

There were 2 key social changes to the lives of women in the Weimar Republic *(p.18)*:

- Young *(p.80)* women had more job opportunities if they lived in a town or city.
- Some women's behaviour changed and they spent more money on clothes, make-up, smoking, drinking and going out.

### What problems were created because of the changes women experienced in the Weimar Republic?

The social, political and economic changes women experienced led to 2 key problems:

- Despite women's rights being protected in the constitution, it did not mean women had equality in reality. For example, women still earned less than men.
- Some people thought women should not be challenging men's roles. For example, trade unions didn't like women workers.

---

**DID YOU KNOW?**

**Compared to many other European countries, Germany had some of the most progressive and equal laws for women in the early 1920's.**

In comparison, Britain did not pass laws regarding equal voting rights for women until 1928.

---

# CULTURAL CHANGES

*The 1920s in Weimar Germany was a time of cultural experimentation.*

### What created the culture change in the Weimar Republic?

There was a revival in culture during the Weimar Republic *(p.18)* which saw people express themselves through art, architecture, cinema and experimentation. This was driven by the new freedoms of the 1920s.

### What was this period of cultural change in the Weimar Republic known as?

The period of revival during the Weimar Republic *(p.18)* is sometimes known by 2 different names.

- Some call it 'the Golden Age' because of the cultural changes.
- It is also referred to by some as 'the Stresemann Era', because it occurred under the leadership of Weimar politician Gustav Stresemann *(p.109)*.

### Why did arts and culture change in Weimar Germany?

There were cultural changes in Weimar Germany due to 4 key reasons:

- Worldwide trends in art and culture and a reaction to the horror of the First World War.
- The country was recovering economically after 1924 so there was more money to spend on arts and culture.
- The political changes the country had experienced as it changed from a monarchy to a democracy allowed for more freedom of expression and speech.
- Several art and cultural movements influenced the change.

### Which movements in the Weimar Republic affected arts and culture?

Cultural change in the Weimar Republic *(p.18)* was influenced by 4 main artistic and cultural movements of the time.

- New Objectivism *(p.41)*.
- Modernism *(p.41)*.
- Expressionism *(p.41)*.
- The Bauhaus *(p.42)* movement.

### How was the art of the Weimar Republic affected by cultural change?

Art underwent a cultural change in Weimar Germany as there were new expressionist artists such as Otto Dix and Otto Müller. Some expressionist painters like Dix and George Grosz painted images which were very negative about life in Weimar Germany. Other expressionists artists produced work that was more spiritual.

### How was the architecture of the Weimar Republic affected by cultural change?

Architecture underwent some cultural change in Weimar Germany as some architects such as Erich Mendelsohn designed buildings in the Bauhaus *(p.42)* style, while Emil Fahrenkamp built modernist *(p.41)* buildings. Both styles rejected all that was considered traditional.

### How was the cinema of the Weimar Republic influenced by cultural change?

Cinema underwent a significant cultural change as film became very popular across the world and technology developed so films using sound, or 'talkies' as they were known, were made. One of Germany's first science fiction films, 'Metropolis', was about life in the 20th century.

### What opposition was there to the changes in arts and culture in Weimar Germany?

There were 2 main groups that were opposed to these cultural changes in the Weimar Republic *(p.18)*:

- Traditionalists criticised these cultural changes because they believed it undermined family values and Germany's traditional way of life. In particular, right-wing political parties such as the Nazis *(p.44)* were highly critical of Weimar culture and saw it as 'degenerate'.
- Many socialists and communists were also highly critical because they believed that the new art and cultural developments only benefitted the middle and upper class, while the working class were still suffering from a lower standard of living.

> **DID YOU KNOW?**
>
> **'Metropolis' was a science fiction film released on 1926.**
> The director, Fritz Lang, made the film, now considered a classic. It depicted a futuristic city that was divided between the privileged and the downtrodden.

# NEW OBJECTIVISM

*New Objectivism is an art form in which life is shown as it really was.*

### What was New Objectivism in Weimar Germany?

New Objectivism was the idea that the arts should show life as it really was and not romanticise it or make it appear better than reality. This idea changed art and culture in Weimar Germany as there was a new focus on real life including poverty and suffering.

# MODERNISM

*Modernism is an art form which looks to the future.*

### How did modernism influence arts and culture in Weimar Germany?

Modernism was the idea that the arts should look to the future rather than the past. This idea changed art and culture in Weimar Germany with a new focus on technology and what the world could look like in the future.

# EXPRESSIONISM

*Alfred Rosenberg, the Culture Minister of Nazi Germany, described expressionism as 'Bolshevik filth'.*

### How did expressionism influence arts and culture in Weimar Germany?

Expressionism was the idea that the arts should express how the artist felt. This idea changed art and culture in Weimar Germany as it demonstrated that art did not have to look anything like reality; instead, it could be an expression of emotions.

## THE BAUHAUS MOVEMENT

*Bauhaus means 'construction house' in English and began in Weimar in 1919.*

**How did the Bauhaus movement influence arts and culture in Weimar Germany?**

The Bauhaus movement was led by a group of designers who focused on a specific style of simple lines and made use of new technology.

## THE DAP

*In 1919, the DAP was a tiny, little known political party in Munich, Bavaria.*

**What was the German Workers' Party?**

The German Workers' Party, or DAP, was a right-wing party that Hitler eventually took over and changed into the Nazi Party (p.44).

**Who set up the German Workers' Party?**

The German Workers' Party was set up by Anton Drexler.

**When was the German Workers' Party set up?**

The German Workers' Party was set up in February 1919.

**What did the German Workers' Party believe in?**

The German Workers' Party had several policies. The 6 main policies included:
- ☑ Policies appealing to workers.
- ☑ Opposition to the Weimar government which it blamed for signing the Treaty of Versailles.
- ☑ Nationalistic ideas.
- ☑ Hatred of the Treaty of Versailles.
- ☑ Hatred of democracy which it thought created weak government.
- ☑ Anti-Semitism.

**When did Hitler join the German Workers' Party?**

Hitler joined the German Workers' Party after attending a meeting as a spy for the German Army on 19th September, 1919.

**How did Hitler take over the German Workers' Party?**

Hitler took over the party slowly. By 1921 he had replaced Anton Drexler as the head of the German Workers' Party.

**How did Hitler change the German Workers' Party?**

Hitler took over and changed the German Workers' Party in 5 main ways:
- ☑ In February 1920, Drexler and Hitler wrote the Twenty-Five Point Programme which stated the party's policies.
- ☑ He increased the membership using his personal appeal and skill as a public speaker.
- ☑ In 1920, the name of the party was changed to the National Socialist German Workers' Party (NSDAP (p.44)) and introduced the swastika and the Nazi salute.

- He officially took over from Drexler as the leader in July 1921, and gave jobs to his supporters such as Rudolf Hess, whom he made his deputy, and Ernst Röhm.
- He created the Sturmabteilung *(p.43)*, or SA, in August 1921, who were nicknamed the 'Brownshirts'. They were the NSDAP's *(p.44)* private army.

## What did the Twenty-Five Point Programme of the German Workers' Party include?

5 of the main policies included in the Twenty-Five Point Programme were:

- They were against the Treaty of Versailles and called for its abolition.
- They had anti-Semitic beliefs, such as no Jew could be a German citizen and only citizens were entitled to a job and a decent standard of living.
- They believed that nationalism would unite all of the German-speaking people, land and colonies to feed the German population.
- The party was against the Weimar Republic *(p.18)* because it was a democracy. The party wanted a strong central government with unrestricted authority and believed democracy weakened Germany.
- They wanted Austria and Germany to unite under Anschluss, which was forbidden under the terms of the Treaty of Versailles.

## How many members did the German Workers' Party have?

Twenty-three people attended a DAP meeting on 12th September, 1919. By the end of 1920, membership had increased to 3,000 people.

> **DID YOU KNOW?**
>
> **3 facts about Hitler joining the DAP:**
> - Hitler was sent by the army to monitor the DAP as they were worried about the growth of revolutionary political parties.
> - Hitler attended a DAP meeting and impressed Anton Drexler when he spoke out against a man who had suggested Bavaria should become independent from Germany.
> - Anton Drexler invited Hitler to speak at the next meeting.

# THE SA

*The SA intimidated the rivals of the Nazis and protected the DAP.*

## What was the SA?

The SA, or Sturmabteilung, which translates as 'storm detachment', was the Nazi Party's *(p.44)* first paramilitary wing.

## When was the SA set up?

The SA was set up in 1921.

## Who joined the SA?

Different groups of people joined the SA:

- Ex-soldiers, especially members of the Freikorps, as they felt betrayed by the Weimar Republic *(p.18)* signing the Treaty of Versailles.
- Unemployed *(p.83)* men, angry with the government.

### How did the SA help the Nazis?
The SA was often violent and disorderly. They regularly disrupted the meetings of other political parties, especially the Communist Party, and beat up the opposition. This helped the Nazis (p.44) become stronger.

### Who was the leader of the SA?
The SA was co-founded and led by Ernst Röhm, a German Army officer. He was a member of the German Workers' Party, and he became a close friend of Hitler.

### What was the SA's nickname?
The SA was nicknamed 'die Braunhemden' - or 'Brownshirts' - because of the colour of their uniforms.

### How many people were in the SA?
By 1932 the SA had 400,000 members, which quickly surged to 2 million after Hitler became chancellor of Germany.

---

**DID YOU KNOW?**

**The SA was not limited by the terms of the Treaty of Versailles.**
The Treaty of Versailles restricted the German Army to 100,000 men. However, the SA had around 3 million men when Hitler came to power in 1933.

---

## THE NAZI PARTY
*Hitler gradually took over the DAP from Anton Drexler and moulded it into his own.*

### What was the Nazi Party?
The Nazi Party was the National Socialist German Workers' Party. It was a extreme right-wing political party and supported the ideology of Nazism, a form of fascism.

### When did the Nazi Party gain power in the Reichstag?
The Nazis gained 32 seats in the Reichstag in the general election held in May 1924. They remained unpopular during the 1920s. In July 1932 the number of seats they held increased to 230. Hitler became chancellor in January 1933.

### What were the main aims of the Nazi Party?
The Nazi Party had 3 main aims:

- The Nazis wanted to destroy the Treaty of Versailles and undo all of the changes it had imposed on Germany.
- They wanted to destroy Weimar's democratic constitution because they saw this as weak. They wanted a strong, central government to make Germany stronger.
- They wanted to expand Germany. They wanted Lebensraum, or living space, particularly in the East.

### What was nationalistic about the Nazi Party?
The Nazis had 4 key nationalistic ideas:

- The Nazis wanted to destroy the Treaty of Versailles to regain all of the territory they had lost.
- They believed in Lebensraum, or living space, to accommodate the nation's population.

- The Nazis wanted to rebuild the strength of Germany's military forces.
- They believed that Aryans were a superior race and only they should be German citizens.

## What was socialist about the Nazi Party ideas?

The Nazis had few true socialist beliefs:

- The Nazi Party claimed it wanted to nationalise industries. In reality, it carried out the 'Aryanisation' of the German economy by seizing business from the control of non-Aryans.
- The Nazis wanted to provide employment for every Aryan man.
- They wanted to give equal rights to all Aryan citizens.
- They wanted to give support to Aryan mothers and children.

## How did the Nazi Party become popular?

There are 4 main reasons why the Nazis become popular in the late 1920s:

- In the early years of the Nazi Party, they kept their policies deliberately vague so they would appeal to as many people as possible.
- Following the economic crash on Wall Street in 1929, the Nazis' popularity rose as they offered to cure the huge unemployment (p.83) issue in Germany through 'work and bread'.
- The Weimar Republic (p.18) once again looked weakened and the Nazis seemed to be the solution, offering a strong dictatorship in its place.
- Hitler appealed to many as he was known to be charismatic and a skillful public speaker. The organisation of the Nazis in their rallies also drew people to vote for them.

## Who funded the Nazi Party?

The Nazis were funded by millionaires, such as Gustav Krupp von Bohlen und Halbach and Alfred Hugenberg. All Hugenberg's 53 newspapers spread the Nazi message.

## How did Hitler help the Nazi Party gain popularity?

There were 5 key ways in which Hitler helped the Nazi Party gain support:

- He was a strong leader and mesmerising public speaker.
- He travelled the country giving rousing speeches.
- Hitler's hatred of Jews struck a chord with many people, as they were seen as a convenient scapegoat for Germany's problems.
- He was seen as their last hope.
- He understood the importance of effective propaganda and created easily recognisable symbols such as the swastika, which he designed.

## What was the Nazi Party message?

Hitler adapted his message depending on his audience. If he was speaking to businessmen, he would talk about how the Nazis would solve the Great Depression. To workers, he said the Nazis would provide employment and food.

## What did the Nazi Party do when they came to power?

Once the Nazis had gained control of the Reichstag, they began to consolidate their power, remove all opposition and create a totalitarian dictatorship in Germany.

### How did the Nazi Party control the legal system?

Once in power, the Nazis abolished trials by jury. All decisions were left to the judges. All judges had to join the National Socialist League for the Maintenance of the Law and take the Hitler oath. Judges were required to rule in the Nazis' favour.

### How did the Nazi Party use censorship?

Once in power, the Nazis used censorship in the following 4 key ways:

- Any books written by Jews, or which disagreed with the Nazi Party's beliefs, were burned.
- All scripts for plays, films or radio (p.77) shows had to conform to Nazi beliefs. Writers were told what to say.
- Only newspapers that supported the Nazi Party and spread their propaganda were allowed to operate.
- Joseph Goebbels, Hitler's propaganda minister, ensured anything which was published conformed to party ideals.

---

**DID YOU KNOW?**

**3 facts about the swastika**
- It was an ancient symbol used in religions, such as Hinduism and Buddhism.
- It was a symbol of well-being.
- Hitler used the symbol along with the colours of Imperial Germany; red, white and black.

---

# MUNICH PUTSCH, 1923

*The failure of the Munich Putsch made Hitler realise he would have to change the Nazi Party to make it electable.*

### What was the Munich Beer Hall Putsch?

The Munich Beer Hall Putsch, was an armed uprising led by Hitler. He planned to establish a dictatorship in the Bavarian city of Munich, with the ultimate aim of overthrowing the Weimar Republic (p.18). It was the last in a series of uprisings that threatened the Weimar Republic between 1919 and 1923.

### When was the Munich Beer Hall Putsch?

The Munich Beer Hall Putsch happened on the night of 8th November, 1923 and the morning of 9th November, 1923.

### What caused the Munich Beer Hall Putsch?

There were 5 main reasons for the Munich Beer Hall Putsch:

- Many people resented the Weimar Republic (p.18) because they blamed the republic for Germany's defeat in the First World War and the government were known as the 'November Criminals' for signing the armistice and the Treaty of Versailles.
- Hitler was inspired by the actions of Benito Mussolini, who had overthrown democracy and set up a dictatorship in Italy in 1922.
- The Nazi Party (p.44) had grown to around 55,000 members in Bavaria by 1923.
- The hyperinflation of 1923 had weakened the Weimar Republic (p.18), so it seemed that it was the perfect time for Hitler to organise a Putsch.

- The former commander-in-chief of the army during the First World War, General Ludendorff, gave Hitler his support. General Ludendorff was very popular in Germany and had a great deal of influence in the German Army.

## What were the main events of the Munich Beer Hall Putsch?

There were 5 key events during the Munich Beer Hall Putsch:

- Hilter took over a political meeting at a beer hall being held by Gustav von Kahr, the leader of Bavaria's state government, von Seisser, the head of the Bavarian police, and von Lossow, the head of the German Army.
- The three men were forced to agree to Hitler's plan of a Putsch at gunpoint. They were then released on 9th November, 1923.
- Under Röhm, the SA *(p.43)* took over the local police and army headquarters.
- On 9th November, Hitler and his supporters marched on the town centre of Munich.
- The police stopped them. Sixteen members of the Nazi Party *(p.44)* were killed and Hitler fled, although he was arrested on 11th November, 1923.

## Why did the Munich Beer Hall Putsch fail?

The Munich Putsch was destined to fail from the offset; here are 3 main reasons why:

- Hitler made several errors - trusting Kahr and Lossow, the two nationalist politicians he planned the revolution with, was one of them.
- The Putsch failed to gain the support needed from the Bavarian people.
- The army also didn't support the movement.

## What were the consequences of the Munich Beer Hall Putsch for the Nazis?

There were both positive and negative consequences of the Munich Beer Hall Putsch in the short-term and long-term.

## What were the negative consequences of the Munich Beer Hall Putsch for the Nazis?

In the short term, there were 2 main negative consequences for the Nazi Party *(p.44)*:

- Hitler was sent to prison for 5 years, but served only 9 months.
- The Nazi Party *(p.44)* was banned and Hitler was forbidden to speak in public until 1927.

## What were the positive consequences of the Munich Beer Hall Putsch for the Nazis?

There were 2 short-term and 2 long-term positive results for the Nazi Party *(p.44)*:

- Hitler decided to use what had happened, and his subsequent trial, to his advantage to gain publicity across Germany, not just in Bavaria.
- Hitler used his time in prison to write his book, 'Mein Kampf', which means 'My Struggle'.
- In the long-term, Hitler realised the Nazi Party *(p.44)* would have to come to power through elections, not by force.
- In the long-term, Hitler would have to re-organise the party.

### DID YOU KNOW?

**Hitler's Putsch was inspired by Mussolini's actions in Italy.**

Mussolini had successfully organised a mass demonstration, called the March on Rome, which resulted him coming to power in Italy in October 1920.

# THE LEAN YEARS, 1924 TO 1929

*Between 1924 and 1929, Hitler reorganised the Nazi Party into a national party that could campaign to win elections.*

### What was done to reorganise the Nazi Party?

The Nazi Party *(p.44)* underwent many changes between 1924 and 1929 when Hitler relaunched it after his release from prison. Hitler used his ideas in 'Mein Kampf' as a blueprint of how to change the party.

### When did the Nazi Party reorganise under Hitler?

The Nazi Party *(p.44)* was relaunched officially on 27th February, 1925.

### Why was the Nazi Party reorganised by Hitler between 1924 and 1929?

Hitler changed and reorganised the Nazi Party *(p.44)* for 2 key reasons:
- To create a party that could appeal to the electorate and win seats in the Reichstag.
- To turn the Nazi Party *(p.44)* into a party that was active throughout Germany and not just Bavaria.

### What was reorganised in the Nazi Party by Hitler between 1924 and 1929?

The following 6 areas were re-organised or changed during 1924 to 1929:
- The headquarters.
- The structure of the Nazi Party *(p.44)* across Germany.
- The creation of the SS *(p.65)*.
- The party finances.
- Propaganda.
- The SA *(p.43)*.

### How did the Nazi Party reorganise their headquarters under Hitler?

The Nazi Party's *(p.44)* headquarters were reorganised in 2 ways:
- Franz Schwarz was appointed party treasurer to improve the finances of the party.
- Philipp Bouhler became party secretary to improve the organisation of the party.

### How did the Nazi Party reorganise the party structure under Hitler?

The structure of the Nazi Party *(p.44)* was changed in 5 key ways:
- The Nazi Party *(p.44)* was organised into different departments, such as a department for industry, with a different person in charge.
- The Nazi *(p.44)* Student League was established - it included the Hitler Youth *(p.80)* to attract the younger generation.
- A women's section was created, called the German Women's Order, to appeal to women.
- The Nazi Party *(p.44)* was organised into 35 different regions across Germany, called a Gau. Each Gau was supposed to have a leader, or Gauleiter.
- A Teachers' League was created in 1929 to appeal to teachers.

### How did the Nazi Party reorganise the party finances under Hitler?

The Nazi Party *(p.44)* raised money from wealthy businessmen such as Krupp, Bosch and Thyssen. This helped finance an increase in propaganda.

### How did the Nazi Party reorganise propaganda under Hitler?

The Nazis *(p.44)* used different forms of propaganda:

- Firstly, Hitler convinced Joseph Goebbels to join the party and he was then employed to revamp Nazi propaganda *(p.72)*. Together they changed tactics and decided to appeal to the majority through several methods.
- They began to use up-to-date technology to broadcast their message. They used radio *(p.77)*, cinema and films.
- They purchased more newspapers, so there were 120 daily or weekly Nazi *(p.44)* newspapers by the 1930s.
- They organised mass rallies. They had one in Weimar in 1926 and then from 1927 onwards they were held in Nuremberg.

### When did the Nazi party set up the SS under Hitler in its reorganisation?

The Schutzstaffel *(p.65)* or SS was:

- Set up in 1925 as Hitler's personal bodyguard.
- Led by Heinrich Himmler.
- Membership increased to 3,000 members by 1930.

### How did Hitler change the SA after 1924 during the reorganisation of the Nazi party?

The SA *(p.43)* was changed in 3 main ways:

- The SA *(p.43)*, or Sturmabteilung, was changed in 1925 as Röhm was replaced by Franz Pfeffer von Salomon as the leader of the SA until 1930.
- It was strengthened with more young *(p.80)* men encouraged to join.
- Its image was improved, placing greater emphasis on discipline and order rather than violence and intimidation.

### What were the results of the reorganisation of the Nazi party under Hitler?

There were 2 key results of the reorganisation of the Nazi Party *(p.44)* between 1924 and 1929:

- They were better organised and were now present in all parts of Germany.
- They only managed to win 12 seats in May 1928, fewer seats than in the 1924 elections, because all extreme parties lost supporters as the Weimar Republic *(p.18)* recovered.

> **DID YOU KNOW?**
> While in prison, Hitler stated that, 'Instead of working to achieve power by an armed coup we shall have to hold our noses and enter the Reichstag .... If outvoting them takes longer than outshooting them, at least the results will be guaranteed by their own constitution!'

# BAMBERG CONFERENCE, 1926

*The Bamberg Conference successfully dealt with splits in the Nazi Party and established Hitler as having absolute power.*

### What was the Bamberg Conference?

The Bamberg Conference was a very important meeting that occurred while Hitler was reorganising the Nazi Party *(p.44)* between 1924 and 1929. Hitler used the conference to establish total control over the Nazi Party.

### When was the Bamberg Conference?
It was held on 14th February, 1926.

### Where was the Bamberg Conference?
It was held in Bamberg in Bavaria. The location was important as it meant that mainly the southern party leaders attended.

### Why was the Bamberg Conference held?
The Nazi Party *(p.44)* was becoming increasingly divided between the north and south. The more industrial areas of the north wanted more socialist ideas to help the workers and were supported by Strasser and Goebbels. However, the southern areas, supported by Hitler, preferred more nationalist ideas.

### What happened at the Bamberg Conference?
There were 2 main events:
- Hitler dominated the conferences. He made the northern 'socialist' members out to be communists who were the enemies of the Nazi Party *(p.44)*.
- Hitler persuaded Goebbels to change his views so that he joined the party's nationalist wing.

### What were the results of the Bamberg Conference?
There were two key results for the Nazi Party *(p.44)*:
- Hitler was now in complete control of the Nazi Party *(p.44)* as he had used the conference to put in place the 'Führerprinzip', or 'Leader Principle'. This meant that Hitler, as the party's leader, was in total control and party members must show total obedience to him.
- The socialist ideas of the Nazi Party *(p.44)* were now no longer as important as its other ideas, such as nationalism.

> **DID YOU KNOW?**
> The Bamberg Conference was important because it was used to eradicate divisions in ideology between northern and southern factions of the party.

# WHY WAS SUPPORT FOR THE NAZIS LOW FROM 1924-1929?
*As Weimar Germany recovered from the hyperinflation crisis, the Nazi Party struggled to win elections.*

### How much support did the Nazis have during the 1920s?
The Nazis *(p.44)* had a low level of support for most of the 1920s.

### What stopped the Nazis getting more support in the 1920s?
There were 4 main reasons why there was limited support for the Nazis *(p.44)* between 1924 and 1929:
- The Dawes Plan *(p.32)* of 1924 helped Weimar Germany to recover economically so people were happier.
- Voters were less likely to turn to extreme political parties because Germany was more stable economically.
- Stresemann's foreign policy meant Weimar Germany's international status had improved so the nationalists were happier.

- In 1925, Paul von Hindenburg *(p.101)* was elected President and, because he was very popular, it helped the Weimar Republic *(p.18)* gain more acceptance.

> **DID YOU KNOW?**
>
> For a question on the value of a source you need to look at three things.
> - ✓ You need to explain what you usefully learn from the content.
> - ✓ You need to consider how the provenance of the source affects its usefulness.
> - ✓ You need to use your own knowledge to prove how useful the source is.

# THE GREAT DEPRESSION, 1930S

*The Great Depression had such terrible effects on Germany that the voters turned to extremist parties for solutions.*

### What was the Great Depression in Germany?

The Great Depression was a world-wide economic depression between 1929 and 1939. It caused mass unemployment *(p.83)* and terrible suffering.

### Why did the Great Depression have an effect on Weimar Germany?

The Great Depression affected Germany for 7 key reasons:
- American banks and businesses had loaned money to Germany under the terms of the Dawes Plan *(p.32)* in 1924. This connected America's economy directly to Germany's.
- German banks suffered terrible losses because they were investors on the US stock exchange on Wall Street.
- Ordinary people panicked about their savings in the banks and rushed to withdraw them. This caused some banks to run out of money.
- German industry and businesses were affected because the collapsed German banks demanded they pay back any bank loans.
- As a result, businesses, farms and industry had less money and had to reduce production or close. Both led to job losses.
- After the Wall Street Crash, US banks and businesses recalled the loans they had made to Weimar Germany.
- Businesses were closing all over the world, which meant there was lower demand for goods, which led to businesses laying off workers. By January 1933, there were 6.1 million Germans unemployed *(p.83)*.

### What were the economic effects of the Great Depression on Weimar Germany?

The Great Depression had 7 key economic consequences for Germany:
- Industrial production fell rapidly as demand for goods dropped. Between 1929 and 1932, industrial production fell by 40% and world trade dropped by approximately 70%.
- Unemployment *(p.83)* increased rapidly. In September 1929, Germany had 1.3 million people unemployed. This increased to 6.1 million by January 1933.
- As the number of unemployed *(p.83)* people increased, the government struggled to pay their benefits. They reduced unemployment benefits, which meant people suffered even more.
- People who had jobs also struggled as taxes were increased to help pay for those who were unemployed *(p.83)*. Wages were also cut.

- Homelessness increased as people could not afford to pay their rent. The combination of unemployment *(p.83)* and homelessness led to more crime and violence.
- The crash of the US stock market affected people with savings who had invested in shares. Their shares became worthless and so too did their savings.
- Everyone was affected, from the young *(p.80)* to the elderly.

## What were the political effects of the Great Depression on Weimar Germany?

The Great Depression had 8 very important political consequences for Weimar Germany:

- The people blamed the Weimar Republic *(p.18)* for the economic problems as they had become dependent on American loans.
- The chancellor between 1930 to 1932, Heinrich Brüning, was nicknamed the 'Hunger Chancellor' because his policies of cutting unemployment *(p.83)* benefits and increasing taxes made the situation worse.
- Brüning struggled to get the different political parties in the Reichstag to pass his laws.
- He asked President von Hindenburg *(p.101)* to use Article 48 to pass emergency laws. Brüning's government increasingly relied on using decrees to pass laws. Approximately 100 decrees were passed between 1931 and 1932.
- The Reichstag couldn't agree on how to solve the economic crisis of the Great Depression and by 1932 it was meeting infrequently. Democracy was failing.
- The extremist parties such as the Communists (KPD) and the Nazis *(p.44)* (NSDAP) increased their share of votes in the September 1930 and July 1932 general elections.
- Between May 1932 and January 1933, the Weimar government was damaged by political intrigue which allowed Hitler to become chancellor.
- Several events involving General von Schleicher *(p.108)*, Franz von Papen and President von Hindenburg *(p.101)* helped Hitler become the chancellor in January 1933 because of the Great Depression.

### DID YOU KNOW?

The governments of Chancellors Bruning, von Papen and von Schleicher were 'Presidential' because they relied on using Article 48, or the presidential power, to pass decrees.

# WHY SUPPORT THE NAZIS?

*The secret of the Nazi appeal: offer something to everyone.*

## What was the increase in support for the Nazi Party?

Support for the Nazi Party *(p.44)* increased because of the effects of the Great Depression on Weimar Germany.

## When did support for the Nazi Party increase?

Support for the Nazi Party *(p.44)* increased in the early 1930s, during the Great Depression.

## Why did the support for the Nazi Party increase in the 1930s?

There were 5 key reasons why support for the Nazi Party *(p.44)* increased:

- Unhappiness with the Weimar Republic's *(p.18)* failure to solve the Great Depression.
- Hitler appealed to many voters.
- The tactics of the Nazi Party *(p.44)*.

- ☑ The impact of the Great Depression.
- ☑ The fear of the Communist Party.

### How did the appeal of Hitler help increase support for the Nazi Party?

There were 4 main reasons why Hitler appealed to the voters because:
- ☑ He presented himself as a strong leader who promised to solve the crisis.
- ☑ He promised to restore law and order which was breaking down.
- ☑ He was a powerful speaker.
- ☑ He promised something for everyone.

### How did Nazi Party tactics help increase support for the Nazi Party?

Nazi Party *(p.44)* used 4 main tactics to increase their support:
- ☑ Propaganda was used to target different groups in society with different election promises.
- ☑ They spent a lot of money on propaganda such as posters, newspapers, rallies and speeches.
- ☑ The SA *(p.43)* increased support for the Nazi Party *(p.44)* because they were well organised and disciplined.
- ☑ The SA *(p.43)* attacked the Communists (KPD) whom the middle class and upper class people feared.

### How did the fear of the communists help increase support for the Nazi Party?

The fear of the Communist Party helped increase support for the Nazi Party *(p.44)* for 2 key reasons:
- ☑ Some people were afraid of the Communist Party (KPD) because their support had also increased between 1930 and 1932.
- ☑ The Nazi Party *(p.44)* was anti-communist so more people supported them.

### How did the failings of the Weimar Republic help increase support for the Nazi Party?

The failures of the Weimar Republic *(p.18)* helped increase support for the Nazi Party *(p.44)* for 4 key reasons:
- ☑ They had failed to solve the crisis of the Great Depression.
- ☑ During the crisis, the weaknesses of the constitution were highlighted as no one party could gain a majority in the elections and the coalition governments kept collapsing on a regular basis.
- ☑ The policies of the Weimar government made the situation worse. For example, Chancellor Brüning had cut unemployment *(p.83)* benefit at the same time as increasing taxes.
- ☑ The method of focusing on the problems of the current government, rather than the positive policies of the Nazi party *(p.44)*, is known as "negative cohesion".

### How did the Great Depression help increase support for the Nazi Party?

The Great Depression helped increase support for the Nazi Party *(p.44)* for 3 key reasons:
- ☑ There were 6.1 million people unemployed *(p.83)* and 17 million relying on benefits. The Nazis *(p.44)* promised them 'work and bread'.
- ☑ The terrible suffering encouraged people to turn to the extremist parties, like the Nazis *(p.44)*, as they searched for a solution.
- ☑ The moderate political parties seemed unable to solve the crisis.

### Which groups increased their support for the Nazi Party?

Many different groups supported the Nazi Party *(p.44)* in the 1930s:
- ☑ Big businesses.
- ☑ Some working class people.
- ☑ The middle classes.

- ✓ Farmers.
- ✓ Young *(p.80)* people supported them because the Nazi Party *(p.44)* appeared exciting with its rallies and the SA *(p.43)*.
- ✓ Some women.

### Why did big business increase its support for the Nazi Party?

There were 3 main reasons why big businesses supported the Nazi Party *(p.44)*:

- ✓ The Nazis *(p.44)* promised to protect them from the communists who would take their businesses away from them.
- ✓ Hitler promised strong leadership.
- ✓ Hitler's plans to use factories to build weapons, battleships and fighter planes meant more money for them.

### Why did the working class increase support for the Nazi Party?

Some working class people supported the Nazi Party *(p.44)* because:

- ✓ The Nazis *(p.44)* promised 'work and bread' for all, which attracted unemployed *(p.83)* people.
- ✓ However, working class people tended to support the communists more.

### Why did the middle class increase support for the Nazi Party?

There were 4 main reasons why many middle class people supported the Nazi Party *(p.44)*:

- ✓ The Nazis *(p.44)* promised to solve the crisis of the Great Depression which the Weimar government appeared incapable of doing.
- ✓ The Nazis *(p.44)* promised to bring back law and order which they felt had broken down with increasing violence on the street.
- ✓ The Nazis *(p.44)* promised to protect them from the communists who wanted to take away their private property.
- ✓ Many middle class people still felt bitter that they had lost their savings in the 1923 hyperinflation crisis and blamed the Weimar Republic *(p.18)* for their suffering.

### Why did farmers increase support for the Nazi Party?

There were 3 key reasons why many farmers supported the Nazi Party *(p.44)*:

- ✓ They promised protection from the communists who they feared would take away their land.
- ✓ The Nazis *(p.44)* promised they would confiscate land from Jewish people and redistribute it to them.
- ✓ The Nazis *(p.44)* promised higher prices for their crops. Prices had fallen because of the Great Depression, and farmers felt the Weimar Republic *(p.18)* had failed to help them.

### Why did women increasingly support the Nazi Party?

There were 3 key reasons why some women supported the Nazi Party *(p.44)*:

- ✓ They promised to solve the economic crisis.
- ✓ They supported traditional values, such as women staying at home and having children, which appealed to some.
- ✓ Some women felt that over the past ten years the youth *(p.80)* had been corrupted by Weimar culture. *(p.39)*

# ELECTION RESULTS
*The Nazi Party election results reflect how strong the Weimar Republic was at that time.*

### Which elections did the Nazi Party take part in?
The Nazi Party *(p.44)* took part in a number of general elections before Hitler became chancellor. These were in May 1924, December 1924, May 1928, September 1930, July 1932 and November 1932.

### What was the importance of the Nazi Party's election results?
The election results show that support for the Nazis *(p.44)* changed depending on how popular the Weimar government was, and how strong the economy was. Hitler was not guaranteed support and had to capitalise on occasions when the Weimar government was weak.

### What were the Nazi Party's election results in May 1924?
The Nazi Party *(p.44)* won 32 seats in the May 1924 general election.

### What were the Nazi Party's election results in December 1924?
The Nazi Party *(p.44)* won 14 seats in the December 1924 general election.

### What were the Nazi Party's election results in May 1928?
The Nazi Party *(p.44)* won 12 seats in the May 1928 general election.

### What were the Nazi Party's election results in September 1930?
The Nazi Party *(p.44)* won 107 seats in the September 1930 general election.

### What were the Nazi Party's election results in July 1932?
The Nazi Party *(p.44)* won 230 seats in the July 1932 general election.

### What were the Nazi Party's election results in November 1932?
The Nazi Party *(p.44)* won 196 seats in the November 1932 general election.

> **DID YOU KNOW?**
> The Nazi party became the largest party in the Reichstag in 1932.

# PRESIDENTIAL ELECTIONS, 1932
*Hitler demonstrated he had become a well-known national figure in the presidential elections.*

### What happened in the presidential election in 1932?
The presidential elections in 1932 saw Adolf Hitler *(p.102)* try to become president of the Weimar Republic *(p.18)*.

### When was the presidential election of 1932?

There were two rounds to the presidential election of 1932. The first round was in March, but as no candidate won 50% of the vote there was a second round in April.

### Who were the candidates in the presidential election of 1932 in Germany?

The three main candidates were: President Paul von Hindenburg *(p.101)*, standing for re-election; Adolf Hitler *(p.102)*, leader of the Nazi Party *(p.44)* (NSDAP); and Ernst Thälmann, leader of the Communist Party (KPD).

### What were the results of the presidential election of 1932?

The results of the two rounds were:

- March 1932: Hindenburg *(p.101)*, 18 million votes (49.6%); Hitler, 11 million votes (30%); Thälmann, 5 million votes (14%).
- April 1932: Hindenburg *(p.101)*, 19 million votes (53%); Hitler, 13 million votes (36%); Thälmann, 4 million votes (11%).

### Why was the presidential election of 1932 in Weimar Germany important?

The presidential election was important because it showed how popular Hitler was. He increased his profile by travelling around the country to give speeches.

---

**DID YOU KNOW?**

**The presidential election campaign was fraught with violence.**
There were frequent clashes between the SA and the Communist Party, which left many people injured and some dead.

---

# HOW DID HITLER BECOME CHANCELLOR?

*Hitler became chancellor of Germany mainly because of the Great Depression.*

### What did Hitler do to become chancellor of Germany?

Hitler became chancellor of Germany because he was able to take advantage of the political and economic crises that had befallen Germany.

### How did Hitler become chancellor?

There were 3 main ways in which Hitler became chancellor of Germany:

- The Nazis *(p.44)* rose to popularity during the Great Depression, having taken advantage of rising unemployment *(p.83)* to gain votes.
- Hitler also took initiative within the political intrigue caused by General von Schleicher *(p.108)*, Franz von Papen and President von Hindenburg *(p.101)* to achieve the chancellorship.
- These showcased that the Nazis *(p.44)* and their leader were quick to react to opportunity.

### When did Hitler become the chancellor of Germany?

Hitler became chancellor of Germany on 30th January, 1933.

## Why did Hitler become the chancellor of Germany?

There are 5 key reasons why Hitler became chancellor:

- ☑ The Nazi Party *(p.44)* increased its number of seats in the Reichstag to 230 in July 1932 to become the biggest party in the Reichstag.
- ☑ The actions of General von Schleicher *(p.108)*, an army general and Franz von Papen, a politician.
- ☑ Without von Schleicher and von Papen, Hitler may not have become chancellor because he did not have enough seats in the Reichstag. They thought they could control Hitler.
- ☑ The failure of the Weimar government to solve the crisis of the Great Depression.
- ☑ Funding from big business that meant the Nazis *(p.44)* could spend a lot of money on propaganda.

## Who helped Hitler become the chancellor of Germany?

There were 3 key men involved with Hitler becoming chancellor:

- ☑ General von Schleicher *(p.108)*, a high ranking army officer.
- ☑ Franz von Papen, a politician.
- ☑ President von Hindenburg *(p.101)* of the Weimar Republic *(p.18)*.

## What role did General von Schleicher play in Hitler becoming chancellor?

General von Schleicher *(p.108)* interfered with the dismissal and appointment of who was chancellor between May 1932 and January 1933 in the following 5 key ways:

- ☑ On 20th May 1932, von Schleicher persuaded President von Hindenburg *(p.101)* to appoint von Papen as chancellor.
- ☑ The new government did not have the support of the majority of the Reichstag.
- ☑ The number of seats won by the Nazis *(p.44)* dropped to 196 in November 1932 but they were still the largest party. Von Schleicher persuaded the president to sack von Papen and appointed Schleicher as chancellor on 2nd December.
- ☑ Von Papen now plotted with Hitler against von Schleicher.
- ☑ Von Papen persuaded President von Hindenburg *(p.101)* to sack von Schleicher and appoint Hitler as chancellor on 30th January, 1933.

## What role did Franz von Papen play in Hitler becoming chancellor?

Franz von Papen helped Hitler by interfering with the appointment of who would be chancellor and plotting with Hitler in 8 key ways:

- ☑ General von Schleicher *(p.108)* persuaded President von Hindenburg *(p.101)* to appoint von Papen as chancellor on 20th May, 1932.
- ☑ This new government did not have the support of the majority of the Reichstag.
- ☑ Von Papen's government struggled and he called new elections in July 1932, in which the Nazis *(p.44)* won 230 seats, making them the largest party in the Reichstag.
- ☑ Hitler demanded von Papen be sacked and himself be appointed chancellor.
- ☑ He called for new elections in November 1932. The number of seats won by the Nazis *(p.44)* dropped to 196 but they were still the largest party.
- ☑ Von Schleicher persuaded the president to sack von Papen and appointed Schleicher as chancellor on 2nd December, 1932.
- ☑ Von Papen told the president that von Schleicher was planning a military coup.
- ☑ He persuaded the president to sack von Schleicher and appoint Hitler as chancellor as he believed he could control him.

## What role did President von Hindenburg play in Hitler becoming chancellor?

President Paul von Hindenburg *(p.101)* helped Hitler become chancellor in 5 key ways:

- He allowed himself to be persuaded by General von Schleicher *(p.108)* to appoint Franz von Papen as chancellor in May 1932. The Nazis *(p.44)* were part of this government.
- He allowed himself to be persuaded by General von Schleicher *(p.108)* to sack von Papen as chancellor in November, 1932 and appoint von Schleicher in von Papen's place on 2nd December, 1932.
- He believed the rumours that Chancellor von Schleicher was planning a military coup.
- He was persuaded by von Papen to sack von Schleicher as chancellor on 30th January, 1933 and appoint Hitler to the role.
- He did not want Hitler to be chancellor but he had little choice. He thought he could control him by limiting the number of Nazis *(p.44)* allowed in the cabinet.

### What role did big business play in Hitler becoming chancellor?

Big business helped Hitler become chancellor when, in December 1932, 39 businessmen wrote a letter to President von Hindenburg *(p.101)* demanding his appointment to save the country from the communists.

# REICHSTAG FIRE, FEB 1933

*The Reichstag Fire enabled the Nazis to blame the communists and declare a state of emergency.*

### What was the Reichstag Fire?

The Reichstag Fire was an arson attack on the German parliament in Berlin - the Reichstag building. Hitler used the attack as an excuse to severely curtail civil liberties and restrict the activities of the Communist Party.

### When did the Reichstag Fire happen?

The Reichstag Fire happened on 27th February, 1933.

### Who was involved with the Reichstag Fire?

A Dutch communist called Marinus van der Lubbe was accused of starting the arson attack.

### What were the results of the Reichstag Fire?

There were 6 key consequences of the Reichstag Fire.
- Van der Lubbe was put on trial and executed.
- 4,000 communists were arrested.
- Hitler persuaded President von Hindenburg *(p.101)* to declare a state of emergency and use Article 48.
- Hitler issued the Decree for the Protection of the People and the State *(p.59)* which ended people's civil rights.
- Hitler announced a new general election for 5th March, 1933.
- Hitler was able to use this increase in his powers to attack his greatest rival, the Communist Party.

### Why was the Reichstag Fire important?

The Reichstag Fire was important for 4 main reasons:
- The Reichstag Fire enabled Hitler to persuade President Hindenburg *(p.101)* that communists were a danger to the country.
- Hitler was able to rule using decrees through Article 48 and he used that power to end people's civil rights. This meant he had increased his powers.
- It meant Hitler could introduce measures that banned leading communists from taking part in the upcoming election campaign.

- This was important because Hitler at this point still did not have the seats in the Reichstag he needed to form a majority.

### What happened to Van Der Lubbe after the Reichstag Fire?
Marinus van der Lubbe was put on trial and executed.

### What happened to communists after the Reichstag Fire?
There were 3 key consequences for the communists:
- The Decree for the Protection of the People and the State *(p.59)* enabled Hitler to ban them from participating in the March election.
- They were targeted, rounded up and arrested with 4,000 thrown in prison.
- All their newspapers were shut down, preventing them from campaigning in the election.

### What decree was created after the Reichstag Fire?
The Reichstag Fire led to the creation of the Decree for the Protection of the People and the State *(p.59)*, which ended people's civil rights and meant Hitler could remove all opposition.

> **DID YOU KNOW?**
>
> **3 facts about the Reichstag Fire:**
> - Some believe the Nazis started the fire using a tunnel between the Reichstag and a neighbouring building which was the official residence of Hermann Göring.
> - The German parliament had to move to the Kroll Opera House.
> - Hitler used the fire to persuade President von Hindenburg that the communists were planning a revolution.

# DECREE FOR THE PROTECTION OF THE PEOPLE AND THE STATE, MARCH 1933

*The decree suspended all civil rights in Weimar Germany.*

### What was the Decree for the Protection of the People and the State?
The Decree for the Protection of the People and the State allowed Hitler to suspend the civil rights of all citizens. The decree also removed all restraints on police investigations which meant people could be arrested and imprisoned without evidence.

### When was the Decree for the Protection of the People and the State signed?
The Decree for the Protection of the People and the State was signed on 28th February, 1933.

### What were the results of the Decree for the Protection of the People and the State?
There were 3 main results of the Decree for the Protection of the People and the State:
- The Nazis *(p.44)* had the power to repress all political opposition through arrests, shutting down meetings, and banning publications.
- They specifically targeted the Communist Party to remove them as rivals in the upcoming March election.

- ✓ It was the beginning of the end of democracy in Germany.

> **DID YOU KNOW?**
>
> The Decree for the Protection of the People and the State is also known as the Reichstag Fire Decree.

# MARCH ELECTIONS, 1933

*The Nazis had hoped they would achieve a majority in the March, 1933 general election, but failed to do so.*

### What were the results of the March 1933 general election?

The Nazi Party *(p.44)* increased the number of seats it held in the Reichstag to 288.

### What happened in the run up to the March 1933 general election in the Weimar Republic?

The Nazi *(p.44)* government used the Decree for the Protection of the People and the State *(p.59)* to arrest communists and ban their newspapers. Hitler persuaded industrialists like Krupp to donate large sums of money to the Nazi Party's election campaign.

### Why was the March 1933 election in Weimar Germany important?

The March election was important for 4 key reasons:

- ✓ The Nazis *(p.44)* didn't secure the majority that they needed in the March elections so they needed the support of other parties to pass legislation.
- ✓ The Communist Party were banned from the 81 seats they had won in the March election by Hitler's emergency powers.
- ✓ The Nazi Party *(p.44)* gained the support of the National Party, which had 52 seats, and the Centre Party (ZP), which had 74, by promising to protect the interests of the Catholic Church.
- ✓ This gave the Nazi Party *(p.44)* the majority it needed to pass laws and, more importantly, to gain 2/3 of the seats that they needed to successfully alter the constitution.

> **DID YOU KNOW?**
>
> **3 facts about the March 1933 general election**
> - ✓ It was the last election that was held democratically.
> - ✓ There was high voter turnout at approximately 89%.
> - ✓ Many middle class people and Catholics voted for the Nazis as they feared the Communist Party.

# ENABLING ACT, MARCH 1933

*The Enabling Act was a large step towards dictatorship in Germany.*

### What was the Enabling Act?

The Enabling Act was a law that enabled Hitler and the Nazis *(p.44)* to pass laws without consulting the Reichstag for a period of four years.

### When was the Enabling Act passed to get Hitler into power?

The Enabling Act was passed on 23rd March, 1933.

### How did the Enabling Act help get Hitler into power?

There were 2 tactics used by the Nazis *(p.44)* to pass the Enabling Act:

- The Nazi *(p.44)* government was able to pass the act by gaining the support of the Centre Party (ZP) and the German National People's Party (DNVP) so that they had the two-thirds majority needed in the Reichstag to change the constitution.
- They also used violence and intimidation to ensure members of the Reichstag supported them.

### What were the results of the Enabling Act for Hitler's power?

Hitler used the power of the Enabling Act to create his dictatorship by removing any opposition from other political parties, trade unions, local government and the army.

### Why was the Enabling Act important for Hitler's power?

The Enabling Act was important because it, in effect, ended democracy in Germany. Hitler used his new powers to remove all possible opposition.

> **DID YOU KNOW?**
>
> **3 facts about the Enabling Act**
> - ✓ The SA were placed in the Reichstag (sitting in the Kroll Opera House) to intimidate members of parliament to vote for the Enabling Act.
> - ✓ The Nazis prevented the Communist Party and some Social Democrats from taking their seats.
> - ✓ It prevented the Reichstag from opposing the Nazi government.

# CREATING A DICTATORSHIP

*Hitler cleverly used the powers of the Enabling Act (1933) to dismantle democracy in Weimar Germany.*

### What did Hitler do to create a dictatorship?

Hitler consolidated his power by creating a dictatorship. He used the Reichstag Fire *(p.58)* to gain the power he needed to be able to pass the Enabling Act in March 1933. This law enabled him to remove all groups, institutions or organisations that could oppose him.

## When did Hitler create a Nazi dictatorship?

Hitler created his dictatorship and consolidated his power between January 1933 and August 1934.

## What did Hitler do to create a dictatorship?

There were 10 main steps that Hitler took to create a Nazi *(p.44)* dictatorship and consolidate his power:

- He used the Reichstag Fire *(p.58)* to gain emergency powers under the Decree for the Protection of the People and the State *(p.59)* which suspended all civil rights.
- He used this power to attack his rivals, the Communist Party.
- After the March 1933 election, he gained the support of the Centre Party and the German National People's Party to achieve a 2/3 majority in the Reichstag so he could pass the Enabling Act.
- Nazi *(p.44)* officials were put in charge of all local government on 7th April, 1933.
- All independent trade unions were banned and replaced with the Nazi *(p.44)* German Labour Front *(p.84)* on 2nd May, 1933.
- The 'Law against the Formation of the New Parties' was passed on 14th July, 1933 which made all political parties illegal except the Nazi Party *(p.44)*.
- In January 1934, all local governments were taken over (regional Länder parliaments were abolished) and Hitler appointed governors to run them instead.
- During the Night of Long Knives, on 30th June, 1934, Hitler had the SS *(p.65)* murder possible rivals in the SA *(p.43)*.
- When President von Hindenburg *(p.101)* died on 2nd August, 1934, Hitler declared himself Germany's Führer, a role that combined the powers of the chancellor and the president.
- The army then swore an oath of loyalty to Hitler.

## How did Hitler control the trade unions in his dictatorship?

Hitler controlled the trade unions through 3 main modes of suppression:

- He banned all independent trade unions on 2nd May, 1933 and replaced them with the Nazi *(p.44)* German Labour Front *(p.84)* to control the workers.
- Workers could no longer complain about pay and conditions or go on strike.
- Trade union leaders were thrown in jail.

## How did Hitler control political parties in his dictatorship?

Hitler also controlled political parties through 3 main modes of suppression:

- The 'Law against the Formation of the New Parties' was passed on 14th July, 1933 and this made all political parties, except the Nazi Party *(p.44)*, illegal.
- Now, the Nazis *(p.44)* could round up all political opposition, arrest them and put them in concentration camps.
- All other political parties were closed down, including their newspapers.

## How did Hitler control local government in his dictatorship?

Hitler controlled local governments in 3 key ways:

- By April 1933, Hitler's puppet local governments were in charge of the local police forces. The Gestapo *(p.66)* was formed and the first concentration camp *(p.67)* for political prisoners opened in Dachau.
- In January 1934, the Nazis *(p.44)* took control of all regional, or Länd, governments by abolishing the regional, or Länder, parliaments.
- Hitler appointed governors who answered directly to him to run the regions instead.

### What did Hitler do to the role of president in his dictatorship?

When President von Hindenburg (p.101) died on 2nd August, 1934, Hitler declared himself Germany's Führer. It was a role that combined the powers of the chancellor and the president.

# THE NIGHT OF THE LONG KNIVES, JUNE 1934

*Night of the Long Knives, or Operation Hummingbird, removed any internal opposition in the Nazi Party to Hitler.*

### What was the Night of the Long Knives?

The Night of the Long Knives was the deliberate and organised murder of Nazi (p.44) and SA (p.43) leaders that the Führer believed posed a threat to his position. The killings were carried out by the SS (p.65).

### When was the Night of the Long Knives?

The Night of the Long Knives began on 30th June, 1934 and continued until 2nd July.

### Why did the Night of the Long Knives happen?

There were 4 main reasons why the Night of the Long Knives occurred:

- Ernst Röhm had become too powerful with 3 million SA (p.43) loyal to him. Röhm was a potential rival to Hitler's position.
- Röhm was very critical of Hitler's policies of working with rich businessmen and the army. He wanted the Nazi Party (p.44) to focus on socialist policies to support the working classes, not on policies which would benefit the businessmen.
- Heinrich Himmler and Reinhard Heydrich, the leaders of the SS (p.65), disliked Röhm and wanted to undermine him. They resented the influence Röhm had over the party, so they told Hitler that Röhm was plotting to seize power.
- The German Army saw the SA (p.43) as a threat because they believed the SA wanted to take over the army, which was a much smaller force of only 100,000 soldiers.

### Who was killed during the Night of the Long Knives?

At the end of the Night of the Long Knives about 400 people had been murdered. These included Ernst Röhm (leader of the SA (p.43)), General von Schleicher (p.108) (the ex-chancellor) and Gregor Strasser (a former leading member of the Nazi Party (p.44)).

### What were the results of the Night of the Long Knives?

There were 4 main results of the Night of the Long Knives:

- Approximately 400 people close to Hitler, who had been regarded as a threat, were now dead.
- The SS (p.65), led by Himmler, emerged more powerful and they, along with Gestapo (p.66), now formed the basis of the police state.
- The SA (p.43) was never again a leading force.
- Hitler got away with having his opposition openly murdered. This established a pattern for the Nazi (p.44) dictatorship.

> **DID YOU KNOW?**
>
> **Röhm was given the option to commit suicide.**
> This was seen as a special privilege because he had such a senior role within the Nazi party. He refused, stating: 'If am to be killed, let Adolf do it himself'.

# THE POLICE STATE
*The Nazi Police State controlled the people through fear and intimidation.*

### What was the Nazi police state?
A police state is one in which the police have absolute power to arrest and punish anyone. In Nazi *(p.44)* Germany, the SS *(p.65)* had absolute power and could arrest, imprison and execute people without trial.

### When was the Nazi police state created?
Hitler began to create the Nazi *(p.44)* police state as soon as he became chancellor in January 1933.

### Why was the Nazi police state created?
The Nazi *(p.44)* police state was created to control the population to ensure their compliance. It used fear to ensure people did not oppose the Nazi government.

### What was the structure of the Nazi police state?
The Nazi *(p.44)* police state consisted of 5 main organisations:
- ☑ The SS *(p.65)*, or Schutzstaffel - German for 'protection squad' - who ran the secret police *(p.66)* and the concentration camps.
- ☑ The Gestapo *(p.66)*, or Secret State Police, that dealt with any opposition to the Nazis *(p.94)* or the government.
- ☑ The SD *(p.66)*, or Sicherheitsdienst des Reichsführers, which was Nazi *(p.44)* Germany's security service. It spied on opponents and critics of the Nazis.
- ☑ The concentration camps, which were used as prisons for anyone who opposed the Nazis *(p.44)* or did something the Nazis disliked.
- ☑ The legal system, which included the judges, courts and lawyers.

> **DID YOU KNOW?**
>
> Those arrested by the Gestapo were forced to sign Form D-11 or an 'Order For Protective Custody', in which they agreed to go to prison.

# THE SS

*The SS were considered an elite force made up of 'racially superior' men.*

### What was the SS?
The SS, or Schutzstaffel, was created as Hitler's personal bodyguard. Its powers were expanded as Hitler created the Nazi *(p.44)* dictatorship and it was responsible for key parts of the Nazi police state. Its members were known as the 'Blackshirts' because of their uniform.

### When was the SS set up?
The SS was set up in 1925.

### Who was the leader of the SS?
The original leader of the SS was Julius Schreck who was appointed in March 1925. However, the best-known leader of the SS is Heinrich Himmler, who was appointed in January 1929.

### How many members did the SS have?
In 1925, there were 250 members of the SS. This figure increased to 240,000 men during the 1930s. The SS had grown to 1 million by 1944.

### Who joined the SS?
Members of the SS had to fit 2 main criteria:
- They had to be examples of the perfect Aryan with blonde hair, blue eyes, tall and physically strong.
- They had to be totally loyal to Hitler because they were his own private army.

### What was the role of the SS?
The SS had 6 roles:
- The SS was in charge of Germany's police force, including the Gestapo *(p.66)*. It had the power to search people's property and send them straight to prison without trial.
- Death Heads - elite groups within the SS - ran the concentration camps and later the death camps.
- The Sicherheitsdienst des Reichsführers-SS *(p.66)* (SD), or Security Service of the Reichsführer-SS, looked after security.
- The Waffen-SS were an elite unit in the army. They were armed regiments that aimed to protect superiors in the SS division.
- It was in charge of racial policies.
- It investigated disloyalty to Hitler in the Nazi Party *(p.44)* and the army.

---

**DID YOU KNOW?**

The SS motto was 'My honour is loyalty.'

# THE GESTAPO

There were around 300,000 members of the Gestapo. They relied on ordinary Germans to inform on their fellow citizens.

### What was the Gestapo?
The Gestapo was Hitler's secret police and established by Hermann Göring. In 1934, the SS *(p.65)* was put in charge of the Gestapo. It was an instrument of terror led by Reinhard Heydrich.

### When was the Gestapo founded?
The Gestapo was initially founded on 26th April, 1933, and transferred to Himmler in April, 1934.

### What was the Gestapo's purpose?
The Gestapo had three main purposes.
- ✓ It spied on German citizens.
- ✓ It prosecuted anyone who spoke out against the Nazi *(p.44)* regime.
- ✓ It created fear. Germans were terrified of the Gestapo because they did not know who its members were.

### How many people were in the Gestapo?
There were only about 32,000 Gestapo. The Gestapo relied on informants to spy on their behalf.

---

**DID YOU KNOW?**

The Gestapo used methods such as blackmail, extortion and planting evidence to secure information.
They also used more physical methods such as torture and sleep deprivation.

---

# THE SD

Sicherheitsdienst des Reichsführers-SS (SD) were the spies of Nazi Germany. They spied on the German people.

### What was the SD?
The Sicherheitsdienst des Reichsführers-SS (SD), or Security Service of the Reichsführer-SS, was the Nazi Party's *(p.44)* intelligence and security service.

### What was the role of the SD security service?
The SD spied on Nazi opposition *(p.94)*, both in Germany and other countries.

### Who was the leader of the SD security service?
It was set up in 1931, by Heinrich Himmler, who appointed Reinhard Heydrich as leader in 1939.

# CONCENTRATION CAMPS

*The Nazis created an extensive system of concentration camps as soon as they took power in 1933.*

### What were concentration camps?

Concentration camps were places where a large number of people were imprisoned and kept in terrible conditions. Nobody could see what happened in the camps as they were in isolated, and often forested, areas.

### When did the Nazis set up concentration camps?

The first concentration camp was set up in 1933.

### Where were the concentration camps?

The concentration camps were in isolated places all over Germany. The first camp was in Dachau.

### Why were the concentration camps built?

Concentration camps were set up for 4 reasons:

- Initially, they were used to imprison political opponents to control opposition to the Nazi *(p.44)* government.
- They were used as a method of control over the population through fear.
- They were used for free labour for the economy. This was particularly important during the Second World War.
- They were used for the mass murder of specific groups of people after 1940 during the Second World War. For example, the Jews were murdered in the Holocaust.

### What were conditions like in the concentration camps?

Prisoners were badly treated, forced to undertake hard labour and ultimately millions were murdered. Those who were unfit to work were sent to the gas chambers during the Second World War.

### Who was sent to the concentration camps?

There were 5 main groups of people sent to the concentration camps:

- 'Asocials', which included alcoholics, homeless people, prostitutes and the 'work-shy'.
- Political prisoners such as communists, socialists and political writers.
- Religious people including Jews, Jehovah's Witnesses and eventually Catholics and Protestants.
- Ethnic groups such as the Jews, Roma or gypsies and, when the Second World War began, Poles and other Slavs.
- Homosexuals.

### What work did prisoners do in the concentration camps?

Within the concentration camps prisoners were made to do hard labour in often freezing conditions.

---

**DID YOU KNOW?**

**3 facts about concentration camps:**

- ✓ The first inmates were political prisoners.
- ✓ There was a prisoner hierarchy which depended on the prisoners ethnicity and nationality with the Jews and Russian prisoners of war at the bottom.
- ✓ Some camps were re-used as prisons by the USSR after the Second World War ended.

# THE LEGAL SYSTEM
*Trial by jury was abolished in Nazi Germany.*

**What methods did the Nazis use to control the legal system?**
The Nazis *(p.44)* took over the legal system by controlling judges, courts and lawyers.

**How did the Nazi regime control the judges in the legal system?**
Judges were controlled in 3 main ways:
- Every judge had to be a member of the National Socialist League for the Maintenance of the Law.
- All judges had to put the interests of the Nazis *(p.44)* above the law and swore an oath of loyalty.
- Any judge that did not become a member of the National Socialist League for the Maintenance of the Law or conform to their expectations, was sacked.

**How did the Nazi regime control the courts in the legal system?**
Courts were controlled 2 key ways:
- Trial by jury was ended so that judges alone decided whether someone was innocent or guilty and determined the punishment.
- The People's Court was set in 1934 to hear all cases that were 'crimes against the state'. Anyone opposing the Nazi *(p.44)* government could not expect to have a fair trial.

**How did the Nazi regime control the lawyers in the legal system?**
All lawyers had to join the Nazi *(p.44)* Lawyers' Association.

**What happened to the death penalty in the Nazi legal system?**
The number of crimes punishable by the death penalty rose from 3 to 46.

---

**DID YOU KNOW?**
The name for the Nazi court was the People's Court.

---

# CONTROLLING RELIGION
*Religion posed a threat to Hitler as the Church was very influential.*

**What did the Nazis do to control religion?**
The Nazis *(p.44)* tried to control religion. They initially worked with both the Catholic and Protestant churches, but after Nazifying church buildings and breaking the concordat *(p.70)* they became enemies.

**What was the role of religion to the Nazis?**
The Nazis *(p.44)* used religion to promote their own ideology and regime. They even attempted to set up a Nazi church called the 'Reich Church *(p.71)*'.

### When did the Nazis try to control religion?

The Nazis *(p.44)* had to first consolidate their power, before attempting to make significant changes to religious organisations. The attacks on German Catholics and Protestants increased dramatically in the 1930s as the Nazis gained more control over society.

### Why did the Nazis want to control religion?

There were 3 main reasons why the Nazis *(p.44)* wanted to control religion:

- Christianity taught love and tolerance which went against Nazi *(p.44)* beliefs. Therefore, religious groups could be predisposed to opposing the Nazi government.
- Religious groups followed the teachings of their religion and their religious leader, eg, Catholics followed the pope, not Hitler.
- Ultimately, Hitler wanted to replace the Church with his own Nazi-based *(p.44)* religion.

### How did the Nazis control religion and the Catholic Church?

Initially, the Nazis *(p.44)* worked with the Catholic Church. Hitler signed an agreement with the pope, called a concordat *(p.70)*, in July 1933. It stated neither side would interfere with the other. However, Hitler broke his promises and attacked the Catholic Church.

### How did the Nazis deal with religion and the Protestant Church?

Initially, the Protestant church worked with the Nazis *(p.44)*. Some members that opposed the Nazis set up the Pastors' Emergency League in 1933. Those that worked with the Nazis created the Reich Church *(p.71)* in 1936, led by Ludwig Müller.

### How successfully did the Nazis control religion?

The Nazis *(p.44)* faced continued opposition from religious groups and were never able to establish total control.

> **DID YOU KNOW?**
>
> Hitler stated in March 1933, 'The national government's concern will be for co-operation of the Church with the state. It expects, however, that [this] will meet with similar appreciation from their side.'

# CATHOLICS

*The Nazis attempted to gain the support of the Catholic Church before they turned on them.*

### What did the Nazis do to control the Catholic church?

Initially, the Nazis *(p.44)* worked with the Catholic Church. Hitler signed an agreement with the pope called a concordat *(p.70)* in July 1933 which stated that both sides would not interfere with the other. However, Hitler broke his promises and attacked the Church.

### Why did the Nazi regime want to control the Catholic Church?

There are 5 main reasons why Hitler tried to control the Catholic Church:

- The Catholic Church had 22 million members, or 32% of the German population.

- It was a very powerful and influential institution which controlled a range of organisations, such as youth (p.80) groups, schools and charities.
- Catholics followed the guidance of the pope as their religious leader. Hitler believed they listened to the pope more than to him.
- Catholics tended to support the Centre Party (ZP).
- Catholics sent their children to Catholic schools and Catholic youth (p.80) groups.

### How did the Nazis try to control German Catholics?

The Nazis (p.44) tried to control the Catholic Church by reaching an agreement with them.

- In July 1933, Hitler signed an agreement with the pope, called the concordat. (p.70)
- In the concordat (p.70), it was agreed that Hitler would not interfere with the Catholic Church or its schools.
- In return, the Catholic Church would not interfere with politics and would swear loyalty to the government.

### How did Hitler break his promises to the Catholic Church in Nazi Germany?

Hitler broke the promises made in the concordat (p.70) by arresting Catholic priests and closing Catholic schools and youth (p.80) groups. He also changed the school curriculum to further reflect Nazi (p.44) ideology.

### What was the pope's response to the Nazi attack on the Catholic Church?

Eventually in 1937, Pope Pius XI spoke out against the treatment of the Catholic Church by the Nazis (p.44) in a speech called 'With Burning Anxiety', or 'Mit Brennender Sorge'.

### How did Catholics respond to the Nazi attack on the Church?

There were 2 main reactions to the Nazis (p.44)' treatment of the Catholic Church:

- About 400 Catholic priests criticised the Nazi (p.44) government and were imprisoned in Dachau concentration camps.
- Catholic Archbishop Galen spoke out against Nazi (p.44) policies and the creation of concentration camps. He was arrested by the Gestapo (p.66) and forced to remain at home for the duration of the Second World War.

---

**DID YOU KNOW?**

**In 1998, Pope John Paul II apologised to the Jewish people for the Catholic Church's failure to speak out against the Holocaust during the Second World War.**

However, no specific criticism was made of the pope at the time, Pius XII, who, according to the Vatican, 'saved hundreds of thousands of Jewish lives himself or through his representatives'.

---

# THE CONCORDAT

*The concordat was an attempt by the Nazis to work with, and control, the Catholic Church.*

### What was the concordat?

The concordat was an agreement between the pope and Hitler, signed in July 1933. It stated that the Nazi Party (p.44) and the Catholic Church would not interfere with one another's policies or spheres.

# THE REICH CHURCH

*The Reich Church followed a Nazified version of Christianity where the cross was replaced by the swastika.*

### What was the Reich Church?
The Reich Church was a Nazi *(p.44)* version of the Protestant Church. It supported the Nazi Party, allowed Nazi flags with the swastika to be hung in their churches and used an altered, Nazified version of the Lord's Prayer.

### When was the Reich Church set up?
The Reich Church was set up in 1936.

### Who was the leader of the Reich Church?
Ludwig Müller was the leader of the Reich Church.

### Why was the Reich Church set up?
There were 3 main reasons for the creation of the Reich Church:
- To unify all of the different Protestant churches into one so they could be controlled more easily by the Nazi *(p.44)* government.
- To be able to promote Nazi *(p.44)* ideas as they now controlled the Reich Church. For example, they tried to stop use of the Old Testament as they saw it as Jewish.
- To prevent Jews from being baptised into Christianity.

### What was the reaction of Catholics and Protestants to the Nazi involvement in religion and the Reich Church?
Initially, the Protestants and Catholics within Germany were not opposed to the Nazi *(p.44)* regime. However, over time opposition grew and some priests began to openly speak out against the Nazis.

# PROTESTANTS

*The Nazis attempted to gain the support of the Protestant Church before they turned on them.*

### What did the Nazis do to control the Protestant Church?
Initially, the Protestant Church worked with the Nazis *(p.44)*. Some of those that opposed the Nazis set up the Pastors' Emergency League in 1933. Those that worked with them created the Reich Church *(p.71)* in 1936, led by Ludwig Müller.

### Why did the Nazis want to control the Protestant Church?
The Protestant Church was the largest in Germany with 40 million members. This was 58% of the population, so it could form a dangerous opposition group. Their Christian beliefs were opposed to many Nazi *(p.44)* beliefs.

### How did the Nazis control the Protestant Church?
The Nazis *(p.44)* used the Reich Church *(p.71)* to control Protestants, by presenting their religious beliefs in a way that supported the Nazi message.

**How did Protestants respond to the Nazi attacks on the Protestant Church?**

The Protestants responded by:

- Some pastors set up the Pastors' Emergency League (PEL) in 1933.
- A new church called the Confessing Church, or Confessional Church, was set up in 1934.
- Some pastors criticised the Nazi *(p.44)* government and approximately 800 were imprisoned in concentration camps.

## THE PASTORS' EMERGENCY LEAGUE

*The Pastors' Emergency League tried to combat increased discrimination from the Nazis.*

 **What was the Pastors' Emergency League?**

The Pastors' Emergency League was set up in 1933 by Protestants who opposed the Nazis *(p.44)*.

 **How did Pastors' Emergency League opposed the Nazis?**

The Pastors' Emergency League (PEL) opposed the Nazis *(p.44)* in three main ways:

- The Pastors' Emergency League (PEL) was created in 1933 and campaigned against the Nazi *(p.44)* government because the Nazis tried to stop Jews converting to Christianity and they wanted to create one national German Christian Church.
- In 1934, it set up the Confessing Church, or Confessional Church, which was against Nazi *(p.44)* interference.
- Pastor Martin Niemöller was a key member of PEL. He was sent to a concentration camp *(p.67)* in 1937 and the PEL was banned.

> **DID YOU KNOW?**
>
> Pastor Martin Niemöller wrote the poem, 'First they came for the socialists...' He was a key member of PEL.

## NAZI PROPAGANDA

*All forms of official media in Germany were controlled by Nazi propaganda and censorship.*

 **What was the purpose of Nazi propaganda?**

Between 1933 and 1945 the Nazis *(p.44)* used propaganda to control what the public knew and to create more support for the regime. The Nazis wanted to influence people's opinions and beliefs to win the hearts and minds of the people.

 **Who was in control of Nazi propaganda?**

Joseph Goebbels was put in charge of the Nazi *(p.44)* government's propaganda in 1933. He was the minister of people's enlightenment and propaganda.

 **What was the main message of Nazi propaganda?**

There were 3 main messages of Nazi propaganda that were repeated continually:

- Blaming the Jews for Germany's problems.
- Criticising the Treaty of Versailles.
- Making Germany great again.

### What was the propaganda strategy of the Nazis?
Goebbels thought propaganda worked best when the people were repeatedly given basic, short messages.

### What methods of propaganda did the Nazi party use?
Between 1933 and 1945 the Nazi *(p.44)* government used 8 different propaganda methods:
- The press and newspapers were under tight control.
- Film was used to push the Nazi *(p.44)* message.
- The availability of radio *(p.77)* was expanded to cover all aspects of people's daily lives.
- Rallies became an annual propaganda event.
- Sport was Nazified to showcase how the Germans were a superior race.
- Literature was used to tell a Nazi *(p.44)* worldview.
- Music *(p.76)* had to be of Germanic roots.
- Art was created to promote Nazi *(p.44)* ideals.

### How was Volksgemeinschaft used within Nazi propaganda?
Volksgemeinschaft means 'national community'. The Nazis *(p.44)* used this idea within their propaganda to encourage people to feel pride for their country and to want to be part of the great German community the Nazis claimed they had created.

> **DID YOU KNOW?**
>
> **The Nazis disrupted films being shown at the cinema that were considered 'un-German.'**
>
> For example, Joseph Goebbels and the SA disrupted the screening of 'All Quiet on the Western Front.'

# THE PRESS
*Joseph Goebbels said, 'If you tell a lie big enough and keep repeating it, people will eventually come to believe it.'*

### What was the Nazi control of the press?
The Nazi *(p.44)* government controlled the press in different ways by censoring information and directing what was published.

### Who was in charge of controlling the press for Nazi propaganda?
Minister of the people's enlightenment and propaganda, Joseph Goebbels, was in charge of the press.

### How did the Nazis control the press?
The Nazi control of the press meant that they could use it for propaganda. This had 4 main outcomes:

- All newspapers that opposed the Nazis *(p.44)* were shut down, and the rest were often told what to write.
- Only the stories that showed the Nazis *(p.44)* in a positive light were allowed to be printed.
- They also used the press to spread negative messages about the Jews. Any editors of Jewish origin were fired and replaced.
- The press was also censored and forbidden to publish certain information.

> **DID YOU KNOW?**
> The Nazi newspaper was called the Völkischer Beobachter.

## RALLIES

*The Nuremberg rallies were the largest and most extravagant of all the rallies.*

### What were Nazi rallies?

Nazi *(p.44)* rallies were organised mass gatherings for propaganda purposes.

### How did the Nazi Party use rallies as a method of propaganda?

In terms of propaganda, the Nazis *(p.44)* had 3 key reasons for organising rallies:
- They were used to celebrate Hitler's greatness.
- To demonstrate how impressive and well organised the Nazis *(p.44)* were.
- To reinforce their control of the people.

### Where did the Nazi Party hold the rallies?

Some of the key rallies were held in:
- Weimar in 1926.
- An annual national rally was held in Nuremberg between 1933 and 1938.

### What were the Nuremberg rallies like in Nazi Germany?

The Nuremberg rallies were the largest rallies that the Nazis *(p.44)* organised. They were held every summer. They included marches of soldiers with flags, torchlight processions and speeches by leading Nazis, with the highlight being speech by Hitler.

### What happened at the Nazi Party rallies?

Alongside the mass rallies there were other events such as bands, speeches, fireworks and air shows.

> **DID YOU KNOW?**
>
> 3 facts about the Nuremberg rallies:
> - ✓ The purpose built rally grounds at Nuremberg covered eleven square kilometers or 4.25 square miles.
> - ✓ The 1934 Nuremberg rally was filmed by Leni Riefenstahl in the movie 'Triumph of the Will.'
> - ✓ Over one million attended the rallies.

# SPORT

*Hitler did not shake hands with any gold winner at the Berlin Olympics, 1936, after the first day.*

### What was the role of sport in Nazi Germany?

Sport was used as propaganda to influence people's attitudes and to increase support for the Nazi *(p.44)* regime.

### How did the Nazi government use sport as a method of propaganda?

The Nazi *(p.44)* government used sport in 4 key ways:

- ☑ They Nazified sport by flying Nazi *(p.44)* flags at all venues, and sportsmen and women had to give the Hitler salute when the national anthem was played.
- ☑ To promote its own ideas of the importance of health and physical fitness.
- ☑ They used the 1936 Berlin Olympics to promote Nazi *(p.44)* rule. A huge new stadium was built, and Hitler used the fact that Germany won 33 medals as evidence that the German race was superior.
- ☑ Leni Riefenstahl filmed the games and her slow motion technique was used as an example of Nazi *(p.44)* brilliance.

> **DID YOU KNOW?**
>
> The 1936 Berlin Olympics was used as propaganda.

# LITERATURE

*Between 1933 and 1945, over 2,500 writers left Germany.*

### What was the role of literature for the Nazis?

Literature was used as propaganda to influence people's attitudes and to increase support for the Nazi *(p.44)* regime. Therefore, literature was controlled by the Nazis.

### How did the Nazi government use literature as a method of propaganda?

The Nazi *(p.44)* government used literature in 5 key ways:

- ☑ The Nazis *(p.44)* controlled literature by banning some books e.g. books by people that the Nazis did not approve of, such as Jews, communists, and anti-Nazis.

- All new books had to be approved.
- 'Mein Kampf' was promoted heavily; for example, it had to be in every school.
- A massive book burning took place in Berlin in 1933, in which books by Jews, communists and anti-Nazis were destroyed.
- Books which focused on glorifying German history or the German race were promoted.

> **DID YOU KNOW?**
>
> **Books were burnt because the Nazis believed they should not be read by Germans.**
> This included books by Helen Keller, Albert Einstein and Ernest Hemingway.

## MUSIC

*Music, like other forms of art and culture, had to be Nazified.*

### What about music in Nazi Germany?

Music was used as propaganda to influence people's attitudes and to increase support for the Nazi *(p.44)* regime. Music, therefore, was controlled by the Nazis.

### How did the Nazi government use music as a method of propaganda?

The Nazi *(p.44)* government used music as a form of propaganda in four main ways:

- Goebbels said music had to be of German or Austrian origin.
- They banned certain types of music such as jazz, which was seen as being influenced by black people, as well as music by Jewish composers such as Mendelssohn.
- Traditional folk and classical music were promoted as being German.
- Marching music, old folk songs and classical music by Bach, Beethoven and Mozart became popular.

> **DID YOU KNOW?**
>
> **Hitler favoured the classical music of composer, Richard Wagner.**
> Hitler even mentioned Wagner in his book, 'Mein Kampf'.

## CULTURE

*Nazis used art and culture to win over people's hearts and minds.*

### What about the arts and culture in Nazi Germany?

The arts and culture were used as propaganda to influence people's attitudes and to increase support for the Nazi *(p.44)* regime. Therefore, the arts and culture were controlled by the Nazis.

## How did the Nazi government use the arts and culture as a method of propaganda?

The Nazis *(p.44)* controlled the arts and culture in 4 main ways:

- ☑ The Nazi *(p.44)* government set up the Reich Chamber of Culture in September 1933.
- ☑ It controlled art, culture, music *(p.76)*, literature, theatre, film and architecture.
- ☑ All art and culture was required to promote Nazi *(p.44)* ideas and give the same message: that all Nazi beliefs and ideas were correct and what Hitler did was in the best interests of the country.
- ☑ Membership was compulsory for actors, artists, musicians and writers or they could not work. Jews were not allowed to become members, and so therefore, could not participate in the arts.

> **DID YOU KNOW?**
>
> Hitler saw modern art as 'degenerate'.

# RADIO

*Radio was a very important form of media to get the Nazi message across to the masses.*

## What about the use of the radio in Nazi Germany?

The radio was used as propaganda to influence people's attitudes and to increase support for the Nazi *(p.44)* regime. Therefore, radio was controlled by the Nazis.

## How did the Nazi government use the radio as a method of propaganda?

The Nazi *(p.44)* government used the radio as a form of propaganda in 5 main ways:

- ☑ The Nazi *(p.44)* government produced a cheap 'people's radio' and 70% of households had one by 1939.
- ☑ All radio stations were censored and controlled by the Nazis *(p.44)*.
- ☑ Speakers were installed in public so everyone could hear the radio.
- ☑ More Germans owned radios than did Americans.
- ☑ Listening to a non-Nazi radio station was illegal. Many tried to tune in to the BBC, but would be taken to a concentration camp *(p.67)* if they were caught.

> **DID YOU KNOW?**
>
> **3 facts about radio.**
> - ✔ Between 1932 and 1939, the number of German families with radios increased from 25% to 70%.
> - ✔ Radio wardens were appointed.
> - ✔ The People's Radio, or Volksempfänger, could not pick up foreign broadcasts.

# FILM

*By 1942, all German film companies were completely controlled by the Nazis.*

### What was the role of film in Nazi Germany?
Goebbels controlled the film industry so that all films supported and promoted Nazi *(p.44)* ideas such as loyalty, self-sacrifice and discipline. They also focused on Germany's glorious past.

### How did the Nazi government control film?
There were 3 main ways by which the Nazis *(p.44)* controlled film:
- The plots and details of new films had to be sent for approval to Goebbels as minister of the people's enlightenment and propaganda.
- The Nazis *(p.44)* made about 1,300 films of their own.
- Films had to have a Nazi propaganda *(p.72)* message e.g. anti-communist or anti-Semitic.

### What films did the Nazi government make?
There were many Nazi *(p.44)* films. These are 3 key examples:
- In 1933, 'Hitler Youth *(p.80)* Quex' was released about a member of the Hitler Youth.
- In 1935, 'Triumph of the Will' was made about the Nuremberg rally. *(p.74)*
- In 1940, 'The Eternal Jew' was made as an anti-Semitic propaganda film.

---

**DID YOU KNOW?**

**3 facts about film:**
- Between 1933 and 1942, film going quadrupled.
- Over 1,000 films were produced during the Third Reich.
- Before the start of the films, propaganda newsreels were shown.

---

# ART

*Hitler had very strong views on art and what was acceptable art in Germany.*

### What did the Nazis do with art?
The Nazi *(p.44)* government controlled artists through the Reich Chamber of Visual Arts, which was part of the Chamber of Culture. Artists had to be members to produce, sell or teach art. All art that wasn't acceptable to the Nazi government was removed from galleries.

# NAZI POLICIES - WOMEN

*For the Nazis, the role of women can be summed up in their slogan: 'Kinder, Küche, Kirche', or 'children, kitchen, church'.*

### What was the Nazi view on women?

The Nazis *(p.44)* viewed women as important as men, but in a subservient role. They believed it was a woman's role to be a housewife and mother. Women should not work but stay home, and their lives should revolve around 'Kinder, Küche, Kirche', or 'children, kitchen, church'.

### What were the aims of Nazi policies towards women?

The Nazis *(p.44)* had 3 main aims for women:
- To give up their jobs.
- To stay at home.
- The most important aim was to have children and raise a 'master race' which would make Germany stronger.

### How should a women look according to the Nazis?

The Nazis *(p.44)* believed women should look natural and the ideal woman would be Aryan. This meant they should wear simple, practical clothes, have their hair in plaits or a bun, and wear flat shoes. Women should not wear makeup or smoke.

### How did Nazi propaganda target women?

Nazi propaganda *(p.72)* targeted women by promoting the message that a women's role was that of a housewife and mother. The perfect women would look natural and have a large family.

### Who was in charge of Nazi policies towards women?

Gertrud Scholtz-Klink was appointed national women's leader of Germany in 1934. She was responsible for implementing the government's policies on women.

### What organisations were set up by the Nazis for women?

The German Women's Enterprise would control the 230 women's organisations that existed in Germany by uniting them into one group. The women's organisations would have to join the German Women's Enterprise or be shut down. The new organisation gave classes on household topics and the skills of motherhood.

### How did the Nazis encourage women to marry?

Women were encouraged to marry by the Nazis *(p.44)*. The party introduced the Law for the Encouragement of Marriage in 1933. This offered loans of 1,000 marks to couples. For each of the first four children, the couple could keep a quarter of the loan.

### How did the Nazis encourage women to have children?

There were 4 key ways in which the Nazis *(p.44)* encouraged women to have children:
- Family allowances were made available to those on low incomes.
- The Nazis *(p.44)* set up the Lebensborn, or Fountain of Life, programme. This involved women having a child *(p.80)* with a member of the SS *(p.65)*.
- Rewards were given to women that had large families. The Mother's Cross was awarded on Hitler's mother's birthday, 12th August. A bronze medal was awarded for four or five children. If a women had six or seven children, she received the silver medal. Gold was reserved for eight or more.
- The law was changed in 1938 to allow divorce if a husband or wife could not have children. This led to an increase in divorce rates by 1939.

### How did the Nazis encourage women to stay at home?

There were 3 main different ways in which the Nazi *(p.44)* regime encouraged women not to work:

- They banned women from entering certain professions. For example, women were forbidden from medicine, working as a civil servant and teaching from 1933 and banned from the legal system from 1936.
- They used propaganda to persuade women to stay home and focus on 'Kinder, Küche, Kirche', or 'children, kitchen, church'.
- Educational opportunities were restricted by controlling the curriculum at school and universities were restricted in how many women they could accept. Only 10% of the enrolled students could be women.

### How effective were Nazi policies towards women?

The Nazi *(p.44)* policies had varying degrees of effectiveness:

- Many women did respond positively to the policies, giving up their jobs and having more children in order to be awarded the Cross of Honour of the German Mother.
- Other women were not entirely convinced, and missed their jobs and other aspects of their pre-Nazi lives.
- However, the effectiveness was nevertheless short-lived when the war broke out in 1939, as there became the need for women to return to work.
- The number of female workers increased from five million in 1933 to seven million in 1939.

> **DID YOU KNOW?**
>
> **There were bridal schools for women in Nazi Germany.**
> Initially, the schools were for women engaged to members of the SS but they were soon extended to suitable Aryan women. They were taught skills of running a household, motherhood and Nazi ideology.

## NAZI POLICIES - YOUTH

*Hitler stated in 1933 that, 'Your child belongs to us already..... In a short time they will know nothing else but this new community'.*

### What was the Nazi view on the young?

Nazi *(p.44)* policy towards the young was focused on shaping the youth into the Nazis of tomorrow.

### What were the aims of the Nazi policy towards the young?

The Nazis *(p.44)* had 3 key aims:

- To create future generations of loyal Nazi Party *(p.44)* supporters.
- To ensure children were strong and healthy so they would produce children of their own.
- To prepare them for their future roles, girls as housewives and mothers, and boys as soldiers and workers.

### What organisations did the Nazis set up for the young?

The Nazis *(p.44)* set up a National Socialist German Students' League.

### When were the Nazi youth groups set up?

The National Socialist German Students' League was formed in 1926.

### When were the Nazi youth groups made compulsory?
In March 1939 it became compulsory for each child to join the relevant Nazi *(p.44)* youth group.

### What Nazi youth organisations were there for boys?
There were different groups set up for boys dependent on their age:
- Little Fellows, or Pimpfe, for six to ten year olds.
- German Young People, or Deutsche Jungvolk, for ten to 14 year olds.
- Hitler Youth, or Hitler Jugend, for 14 to 18 year olds.

### What were the activities for boys in the Hitler Youth during the Nazi regime?
In the Hitler Youth the boys received political training on Nazi *(p.44)* beliefs and views, physical training such as hiking and sports, and military training such as map skills and weapons training.

### What Nazi youth organisations were there for girls?
There were 2 main groups set up for girls, dependent on their age:
- Young Maidens, or Jungmädel, for ten to 14 years olds.
- League of German Maidens, or Bund Deutscher Mädel, for 14 to 21 year olds.

### What activities did young girls do in the League of German Maidens youth group in Nazi Germany?
In the League of German Maidens, girls received political training on Nazi *(p.44)* ideas, physical training such as sports, and training on how to be a mother and housewife, such as learning cooking skills.

### How effective were Nazi policies towards the youth?
Nazi *(p.44)* policies towards the young were partially successful.
- Some children loved the Hitler Youth and fully embraced Nazi *(p.44)* ideals. There are even examples of children informing the Gestapo *(p.66)* about their own parents and teachers.
- Other children weren't as enthusiastic and hated the activities and ideals. The fact attendance of the Hitler Youth had to be made compulsory demonstrates this.
- Some went as far as to actively protest against the regime, such as the White Rose Group *(p.96)* and the Edelweiss Pirates. The Nazis *(p.44)* were clearly unable to indoctrinate all young people in Germany.

---

**DID YOU KNOW?**

**3 facts about the Nazi Youth Groups.**
- ✓ When they became compulsory, children were supposed to have a doctor's note if they were sick and missed a meeting.
- ✓ The uniforms were provided free of charge for some poorer families.
- ✓ The Boy Scouts was banned in Nazi Germany.

# NAZI POLICIES - EDUCATION

*Hitler wrote in 'Mein Kampf', 1924, 'A less educated, but physically healthy individual ...is more valuable ...than an intellectual weakling.'*

### What was the Nazi view of education?
Nazi education policy was designed to make children loyal to the Nazi *(p.44)* regime in preparation for their future roles in the state. Policies in education affected many aspects of young *(p.80)* people's lives.

### What were the aims of Nazi education policies?
The aim of Nazi education policies was to create a new generation of Nazis *(p.44)* loyal to Hitler and believing in Nazi ideas.

### Who was in charge of Nazi education?
Bernhard Rust, who had been a teacher, was appointed education minister in 1934.

### How were teachers controlled by the Nazis education policies?
The Nazis *(p.44)* controlled teachers in 3 key ways:
- The Nazis *(p.44)* passed a law so that they could dismiss any teacher in April 1933. This enabled them to remove all 'unsuitable' teachers from schools.
- All teachers had to join the Nazi *(p.44)* Teachers' Association or League. The League ran teacher-training courses to teach them Nazi ideas.
- Teachers had to swear an oath of loyalty to Hitler.

### How was the curriculum in education controlled by the Nazis?
The Nazis *(p.44)* completely changed the school curriculum in 4 key ways:
- They banned some subjects, such as religious education, and added new ones such as race studies. This taught children about the Nazi *(p.44)* belief in the inferiority of some races.
- All educational books had to be rewritten from a Nazi *(p.44)* point of view. History books glorified Germany's past and taught children that the country's defeat in the First World War was the fault of socialists, communists and the Jews.
- The number of physical education classes was increased, so students had at least five hours of PE a week.
- Girls and boys studied different subjects. Girls had to study 'domestic science' which included cooking and sewing lessons.

### How were the textbooks in education controlled by the Nazis?
All textbooks had to be approved by the Nazis *(p.44)* from 1935. Hitler's book 'Mein Kampf', or 'My Struggle', was made compulsory in every school.

### How were Jewish students treated in education by the Nazis?
Jewish children were regularly humiliated and made to sit at the back of the class, until they were banned from going to school completely in 1938.

### What was the role of the Adolf Hitler Schools in Nazi education?
Any talented boys aged between 12 and 18 were sent to Adolf Hitler *(p.102)* Schools.

**DID YOU KNOW?**

School textbooks books were re-written to teach Nazi ideas.

One maths problems was 'To keep a mentally ill person costs approximately 5 Reichsmark per day and there are 300,000 mentally ill in care. How much do these people cost to keep in total?'

# NAZI POLICIES - EMPLOYMENT

*The Nazi policies on employment did create jobs for those who were unemployed but at a cost of jobs for Jews and women.*

### What did the Nazis do to reduce unemployment?

When Hitler became chancellor there were 6 million Germans unemployed. The Nazis *(p.44)* introduced policies aimed at reducing unemployment, including the Reich Labour Service, rearmament and building projects such as the autobahns.

### Why did the Nazis aim to reduce unemployment?

The Nazis *(p.44)* introduced policies to reduce unemployment because having people out of work was potentially dangerous to Hitler politically and the unemployed were seen as not contributing to society.

### What was the RAD set up by the Nazis and how did it help unemployment?

The Reich Labour Service (RAD):

- It was set up in 1933.
- It gave all unemployed men public work to do, such as maintaining roads and planting trees.
- It paid the men a small amount of money.
- It was compulsory which meant all young *(p.80)* men aged 18 to 25 had to serve for at least six months.
- It was not popular with the young *(p.80)* men because of the low wages and the work was considered to be boring.

### How did the Nazi public works programme help reduce unemployment?

The Nazis *(p.44)* created jobs by setting up a public works programme which included:

- Planting trees.
- Building autobahns (motorways).
- Building new schools and hospitals.
- Building and improving sport facilities e.g Berlin Olympic Stadium.
- Draining marshes to create farmland.

### How did the Nazi autobahns project help reduce unemployment?

Hitler set up the autobahn (or motorway) project in 1933, hoping to build 7,000 miles of roads. By 1935 there were 125,000 men working on the project. It helped by giving unemployed men a job to do and improving transportation links.

### How did Nazi rearmament help reduce unemployment?

Rearmament helped in 3 main ways:

- In 1933, Hitler broke the terms of the Treaty of Versailles by secretly introducing conscription. It was publically announced in 1935.
- There were 1.3 million men serving in Germany's armed forces by 1939.
- This resulted in the growth in supporting industries such as those that made uniforms, weapons and arms.

## What was 'invisible unemployment' under the Nazis?

There were 5 main groups who were classed as 'invisible unemployed':

- Young (p.80) men were not counted when they did their six-month service in the RAD.
- Women who were forced to give up their jobs were not counted.
- Jews who were forced to give up their jobs were not counted.
- People imprisoned in concentration camps were not counted.
- Men conscripted into the army were not counted.

## What were the disadvantages of the Nazi policies to reduce unemployment?

There were 3 key problems with Nazi (p.44) policies aimed at reducing unemployment:

- Invisible unemployment existed. Women, Jews and people in concentration camps were not counted in official unemployment figures.
- The policies cost money and the Nazi (p.44) government was in debt. In 1933, for example, the government spent 18 billion marks on public works; this increased to 38 billion marks in 1938.
- The Nazis (p.44) exaggerated their success.

## What were the positive results of the Nazi policies to reduce unemployment?

There were 5 key positive results:

- According to official government figures, the Nazis (p.44)' policies did reduce unemployment by more than four million.
- Most men who weren't Jewish or in a concentration camp (p.67) were in work.
- Some businesses benefitted from increased investment and opportunities.
- Large businesses benefitted from wage restrictions and there being no trade unions.
- Public works programmes provided better transport, services and homes.

---

**DID YOU KNOW?**

Men in the RAD built the 1936 Olympic Stadium.

---

# NAZI POLICIES - LABOUR FRONT

*On 2nd May 1933, the headquarters of different trade unions were raided by the SA and the police. They were shut down, their leaders arrested and their money confiscated.*

## What was the Reich Labour Front?

The Labour Front, or Deutsche Arbeitsfront (DAF), was the Nazi (p.44) trade union. It was created to replace independent trade unions when they were made illegal by Hitler.

### When was the Reich Labour Front set up?
The DAF was set up in May 1933.

### Why was the Reich Labour Front set up?
The DAF was set up to control workers and employers.

### What organisations were a part of the Reich Labour Front?
The organisations Strength Through Joy and Beauty of Labour were part of the DAF.

### What benefits did the Reich Labour Front bring?
DAF did protect workers, as it set out their rights in the workplace, placed a maximum on the number of hours worked and a minimum on wages.

### What were the disadvantages of the Reich Labour Front?
The negatives of the DAF were that workers lost their right to strike, negotiate their wages and working conditions with their employer, and could be punished if they disrupted production.

> **DID YOU KNOW?**
>
> The Beauty of Labour tried to improve the conditions of the workers.
> Although, the workers often had to do the improvements themselves such as painting and decorating!

## NAZI POLICIES - STANDARD OF LIVING
*Life improved for some in Nazi Germany, but not for all.*

### What happened to the standard of living in Nazi Germany?
Standard of living is a way of measuring whether a person's life is improving or not. It is affected by several factors such as employment, wages and prices. For some people it improved and they benefitted but for others it did not.

### How did employment change the standard of living in Nazi Germany?
Employment affected the standard of living and some people benefitted:
- More people were in work in Nazi (p.44) Germany so they had wages. New jobs were created building autobahns, hospitals and schools, and within the military.
- However, those not in work, like the Jews, did not see an increase in their standard of living and did not benefit.

### How did wages change the standard of living in Nazi Germany?
Wages affected people's standard of living and whether someone benefitted from Nazi (p.44) rule:
- Overall, wages increased compared to 1933; there was a 20% increase by 1939 so that the average weekly wages rose from 86 marks in 1932 to 109 marks in 1939.
- However, it depended on your job. Those in the Reich Labour Service were not paid much.

### How did prices of goods change the standard of living in Nazi Germany?
The price of goods affected the standard of living. Wages increased by about 20% between 1933 and 1939, but so too did the price of food. Therefore, workers did not benefit.

### How did working hours change the standard of living in Nazi Germany?
The number of hours Germans worked each week increased to 49 by 1939; 6 more than in 1933. Thus, workers did not really have a pay rise, and did not benefit.

### How did the Labour Front change the standard of living in Nazi Germany?
The Labour Front *(p.84)* (DAF) impacted the standard of living and whether people benefitted:
- It worked to protect the rights of workers as it placed a maximum on the number of hours worked and a minimum of wages.
- However, workers also lost their right to go on strike and ability to negotiate their wages.

### How did Strength Through Joy change the standard of living in Nazi Germany?
Strength Through Joy (KDF) impacted the standard of living and whether people benefitted:
- It provided cheap leisure activities including films, theatre shows, outings and sports events. Many people benefitted from this.
- However, KDF also meant that people's leisure time was being controlled by the Nazi party *(p.44)*. Some resented this level of interference in their lives.

### How did Beauty of Labour change the standard of living in Nazi Germany?
The Beauty of Labour (SDA) affected the German standard of living and whether people benefitted from Nazi *(p.44)* rule:
- It campaigned for better working conditions and facilities, such as better toilets.
- Workers often had to carry out the improvements themselves in their own time and without being paid for the work they did.

### How did the standard of living change in Nazi Germany?
There is evidence to suggest that some people did benefit from Nazi *(p.44)* rule and their standard of living improved, but many's did not.

### In what ways did the standard of living improve in Nazi Germany?
There were 9 main ways in which the standard of living improved and people benefitted:
- Non-Jewish small businesses benefitted when the Nazis *(p.44)* banned new department stores from opening up as it limited their competition. They were also helped when Jewish businesses were closed down.
- Farmers benefitted as some farm debts were written off.
- Big business benefitted from the government's investment in the armaments industry. They were helped by the restrictions placed on trade union activity.
- Unemployment *(p.83)* was reduced. Unskilled workers gained work through the public works programmes.
- Working conditions improved through the activities of the Beauty of Labour scheme.
- Strength through Joy offered cheap leisure activities and cheap holidays.
- Young *(p.80)* people benefitted from the camaraderie and training provided in the Hitler Youth, as well as an increase in their health and fitness.
- Women's role within the home was respected and Aryan women were given rewards if they had multiple children.
- People accepted giving up some freedoms in return for greater economic stability.

### In what ways did the standard of living not improve in Nazi Germany?

There were 11 main ways in which the standard of living did not benefit the population:

- Between 1936 and 1939 the number of small businesses decreased.
- Farmers objected to government interference and struggled to find enough workers.
- Larger businesses objected to Nazi *(p.44)* interference in all aspects of business life, such as price controls.
- Unemployment *(p.83)* benefit was higher than the wages for unskilled workers so there was little incentive to work. Their working week also increased from 43 to 49 hours by 1939.
- If you belonged to any of the groups the Nazis *(p.44)* persecuted or forced out of a job, your standard of living was much lower.
- Unemployed *(p.83)* men aged between 18 and 25 resented being forced to join the Reich Labour Services. The jobs were difficult and it was run along military lines with a uniform and strict discipline.
- Strength through Joy activities were controlled by the Nazis *(p.44)*. Therefore, people were not free to choose where to go on holiday and activities were limited.
- Many women were forced to give up their jobs and resented this.
- Because trade unions were banned people lost their democratic voice and their ability to influence change in their working conditions. Workers had no rights.
- Food prices went up and there were fewer consumer goods to buy.
- Many people objected to Nazi *(p.44)* indoctrination, and the level of control the Nazis had in their lives.

> **DID YOU KNOW?**
>
> 3 facts about the standard of living:
> - Between 1933 and 1939 workers wages fell.
> - You were not allowed to question your working conditions and could be blacklisted if you did.
> - The number of hours worked increased by 15%.

# PERSECUTION OF MINORITIES
*The Nazis targeted different groups they considered inferior.*

### What was the Nazi persecution of minorities?

The persecution of minorities was the deliberate attack on certain minority groups, or 'undesirable people', such as Jews, Roma (gypsies) or homosexuals. They believed these 'undesirable people' were inferior and persecution escalated over time.

### Why did the Nazis start the persecution of minorities?

The Nazi *(p.44)* persecution of different minorities occurred because of 2 main reasons:

- They believed in eugenics. This is selective breeding to create 'better' humans. The Nazis *(p.44)* believed Aryans should only breed with other Aryans to keep the race strong.
- As they believed that the Aryans were the superior race, they believed they should rule the world and therefore inferior races should be removed.

**When did the Nazis carry out the persecution of minorities?**

The Nazi *(p.44)* persecution of minorities happened between 1933 and 1945.

 **Who were the 'Untermenschen' that faced persecution from the Nazis?**

The Nazis *(p.44)* believed that inferior races were 'Untermenschen', or sub-human, and that they were Lebensunwertes, or unworthy of life. They were part of the 'undesirable people'.

 **Why did the Nazi idea of the Aryan race lead to the persecution of minorities?**

The Nazis *(p.44)* believed there was a superior race, the Aryans, who came from certain parts of Europe. They tended to have blond hair, blue eyes and were physically strong.

 **Why did the Nazis carry out the persecution of the Jews?**

Anti-Semitism means being anti-Jewish. The Nazi *(p.44)* persecution of minorities involved attacks on Jews because the Nazis were anti-Semitic. Hitler blamed Jews for Germany's defeat in the First World War, and they built on existing anti-Semitic feeling that already existed in Germany.

 **Why did the Nazis carry out the persecution of the Slavs?**

Nazis *(p.44)* persecuted Slavic people from eastern Europe because they believed they were 'Untermenschen'. They also wanted to expand Germany into eastern Europe and wanted Lebensraum for Germans.

 **Why did the Nazis carry out the persecution of the Roma?**

Nazis *(p.44)* persecuted the Roma, or gypsies, because they saw them as 'Untermenschen' (sub-human). Roma tended to move around and the Nazis believed they did not contribute properly to society.

 **Why did the Nazis carry out the persecution of homosexuals?**

Nazis *(p.44)* persecuted homosexuals because they believed they were not doing their duty in reproducing.

 **Why did the Nazis carry out persecution of disabled people?**

Nazis *(p.44)* persecuted disabled people because they believed that spending money on them was a waste of resources and, if they reproduced, their offspring would pollute the Aryan race.

---

### DID YOU KNOW?

**Nazi racial policies were based on eugenics.**

The Nazis took the science of selective breeding to an extreme. They believed that there was a 'master race' and by selecting the 'best' Germans to have children they could strengthened this 'master race'

# PERSECUTION OF DISABLED PEOPLE

*Disabled people were the first group to be persecuted in Nazi Germany.*

### What was the Nazi persecution of disabled people?
The Nazi *(p.44)* persecution *(p.87)* of disabled people included anyone in Germany with physical or mental disabilities. The nature of persecution escalated and became worse over time. This was the first group of people to be murdered.

### When did the Nazi persecution of disabled people begin?
The Nazi *(p.44)* persecution *(p.87)* of disabled people started in 1933 and continued until 1945.

### Why did the Nazi regime carry out the persecution of disabled people?
The Nazis *(p.44)* persecuted disabled people because they believed it was wasteful looking after them and if they reproduced, their offspring would ruin the Aryan race.

### How were disabled people targeted by the persecution from the Nazis regime?
There were 3 main attacks on disabled people:
- ☑ The Law for the Prevention of Hereditarily Diseased Offspring was passed in 1933. This led to people being sterilised if they were physically or mentally disabled such as being deaf or blind, or were suffering from a psychiatric disorder such as alcoholism. By 1939, between 200,000 and 400,000 people had been sterilised.
- ☑ In 1939, the Nazis *(p.44)* started the T4 Programme which was the planned murder of those with severe physical or mental disabilities through a massive drug overdose or starvation. It is estimated that more than 5,000 children were murdered under this programme.
- ☑ Many disabled people were also subjected to medical experiments.

---
**DID YOU KNOW?**

The Nazis believed in Darwin's theory of natural selection.

---

# PERSECUTION OF HOMOSEXUALS

*Homosexuals were persecuted, but lesbians were not.*

### What was the Nazi persecution of homosexuals?
The Nazi *(p.44)* persecution *(p.87)* of homosexuals was an attack on gay men. Generally, lesbians were not considered a threat to the Nazi regime. The nature of the persecution escalated over time and became worse.

### Why did the Nazi regime carry out the persecution of homosexuals?
The Nazis *(p.44)* persecuted homosexuals because it was believed they were failing in their duty to reproduce and needed to sexually conform.

### When did the Nazi persecution of homosexuals begin?
The Nazi *(p.44)* persecution *(p.87)* of homosexuals started in 1933 and continued to 1945.

### How were homosexuals targetted by Nazi persecution?

There were 3 main attacks on homosexuals:

- Laws against homosexuality were passed in 1935. As a result the number of men imprisoned for homosexuality increased tenfold from approximately 800 in 1934 to 8,000 in 1938.
- Many homosexuals were sent to concentration camps. It is estimated that about 60%, or 5,000, of all homosexual prisoners died.
- Homosexuals were experimented on in the camps and were castrated.

> **DID YOU KNOW?**
> The leader of the SA, Ernst Röhm, was homosexual.

# PERSECUTION OF ROMA

*Roma or gypsies were targeted because they were seen as inferior by the Nazis.*

### What was the Nazi persecution of Roma?

The Nazi *(p.44)* persecution *(p.87)* of Roma, or gypsies, was the attack on a group of people that were itinerant (moved around) and were considered inferior. The nature of the persecution escalated over time.

### Why did the Nazis target Roma Gypsies for persecution?

The Nazis *(p.44)* persecuted Roma, or gypsies, because they saw them as 'Untermenschen' or sub-human. The Roma tended to move around and the Nazis believed they did not contribute enough to society.

### When did the Nazi persecution of Roma begin?

The Nazi *(p.44)* persecution *(p.87)* of Roma or gypsies started in 1933 and continued to 1945.

### How were Roma Gypsies targetted by Nazi persecution?

There were 6 key stages in the persecution *(p.87)* of Roma, or gypsies:

- After Hitler became chancellor, more Roma were arrested and sent to concentration camps.
- Many Roma, or gypsies, were forcibly sterilised so they could not have children.
- Some Roma, or gypsies, were held in special camps from 1936.
- The Decree for Combating the Gypsy Plague was issued by Himmler on 8th December, 1938. This set up a nationwide database of all Roma. It was used to round up Roma and put them in concentration camps.
- In October 1939, a decree was issued banning the movement of Roma, or gypsies.
- The Decree for the Resettlement of the Gypsies was passed on 27th April, 1940 and aimed to deport all Roma from Germany within one year.

> **DID YOU KNOW?**
> The Nazis murdered around 130,000 Romani Gypsies.

# PERSECUTION OF JEWS

*The Nazis attacked the Jews politically, socially and economically, so as to isolate them.*

### What was the Nazis' persecution of Jews?

The Nazi *(p.44)* persecution *(p.87)* of the Jews was an attack on people of Jewish descendent or anyone the Nazis classed as a Jew. The nature of the persecution escalated and became worse over time.

### Why did the Nazis persecute the Jews?

The Nazis *(p.44)* were anti-Semitic, which is why they persecuted Jews. They considered all Jewish people to be 'Untermenschen', or sub-human. Hitler blamed them for Germany's defeat in the First World War.

### When did the Nazi persecution of the Jews begin?

The Nazi *(p.44)* persecution *(p.87)* of Jews started in 1933 and continued to 1945.

### How were the Jews persecuted by the Nazis?

There were several stages in the persecution *(p.87)* of the Jews. These are 6 of the major events:

- In April 1933, the Nazis *(p.44)* organised a one-day boycott of Jewish shops. Nazi SA *(p.43)* men stood by the doors of the shops to intimidate people so they would not buy goods.
- In 1933, Jews were forced out of jobs in the law, the civil service, dentistry, journalism, teaching and farming.
- In September 1935, the Nuremberg Laws were passed. Firstly, the Reich Citizenship Law stated Jews couldn't be citizens. Secondly, the Law for the Protection of German Blood and Honour made it illegal for Jews to marry non-Jews.
- During Kristallnacht *(p.93)*, the SA *(p.43)* and ordinary Germans attacked Jewish shops, homes and synagogues. Synagogues were burned, approximately 100 Jews were murdered, and 20,000 Jewish men were sent to concentration camps.
- In 1940, all Jews in the countries Germany had invaded were forced to live in concentration camps or ghettos.
- From January 1942, the Nazis *(p.44)* start to prepare the 'Final Solution'. This was the murder of all Jews in Germany, and the lands the Nazis controlled, by working Jews to death as slave labour or by murdering them in concentration camps.

> **DID YOU KNOW?**
>
> **Anti-Semitism was hidden during the Berlin Olympics in 1936.**
> Anti-Semitic signs were removed and Jewish contenders from foreign nations were allowed to participate in the Berlin Olympics.

# JEWISH SHOP BOYCOTT, APRIL 1933

*The SA organised boycott of Jewish shops was the start of organised government attacks on the Jewish community.*

### What was the Nazi boycott of Jewish shops?

The Nazis *(p.44)* organised a one-day boycott of Jewish shops. Nazi SA *(p.43)* men stood by the doors to intimidate people so they would not go inside and buy goods.

### When was the Nazi boycott of Jewish shops?

The Nazi *(p.44)* boycott of Jewish shops happened on 1st April, 1933.

### Why did the Nazis boycott Jewish shops?

The Nazi *(p.44)* boycott of Jewish shops was held to humiliate Jewish people and hurt them economically.

> **DID YOU KNOW?**
>
> The Jewish shop boycott happened only 62 days after Hitler came to power.

# THE NUREMBERG LAWS, 1935

*The Nuremberg Laws were a turning point because they removed the rights of the Jews and their legal protection in the law.*

### What were the Nuremberg Laws?

The Nuremberg Laws were passed to remove the rights of Jews and it enabled the Nazis *(p.44)* to increase their persecution *(p.87)* of Jewish people.

### When were the Nuremberg Laws passed?

The Nuremberg Laws were announced on 15th September, 1935.

### Why were the Nuremberg Laws passed?

The Nazis *(p.44)* brought in the Nuremberg Laws so that they could remove the rights of the Jews as citizens of Germany. As a result, it was easier to persecute them as Jews no longer had any legal protection.

### How did the Nuremberg Laws affect Jewish people's citizenship?

One of the Nuremberg Laws was The Reich Citizenship Law which stated that no Jew could be a German citizen. This meant that Jews were German 'subjects' and they lost their rights to vote or have a German passport.

### How did the Nuremberg Laws affect marriage for Jewish people?

Another Nuremberg Law was the Law for the Protection of German Blood and Honour that made it illegal for Jews to marry or have sexual relations with non-Jews.

> **DID YOU KNOW?**
>
> **After the Nuremberg Laws, the Nazis continued to remove the rights of Jews.**
> - ✓ Jews were banned from public places such as swimming pools.
> - ✓ Jewish children were banned from attending German schools.
> - ✓ Jews had their passports stamped with the letter J.

# KRISTALLNACHT, NOVEMBER 1938

*Kristallnacht was another key turning point as it was the first state organised physical attack on the Jewish community.*

## What was Kristallnacht?

During Kristallnacht (also known as The Night of Broken Glass or Crystal Night), the SA *(p.43)* and ordinary Germans attacked Jewish shops, homes and synagogues. About 100 Jews were murdered, synagogues were burned and 20,000 Jews were sent to concentration camps.

## When was Kristallnacht?

Kristallnacht started on the evening of 9th November, 1938 and carried on into the morning of the 10th November, 1938.

## Why did Kristallnacht happen?

Kristallnacht happened because on 7th November, 1938, a German man, Ernst vom Rath, was shot in the German embassy in Paris by a Polish Jew and the Nazis *(p.44)* used this event as an excuse to attack the Jews.

## What happened during Kristallnacht?

There were 3 main events that took place during Kristallnacht:

- On 8th November, 1938, Goebbels ordered the newspapers to print anti-Jewish stories in Hanover. As a result, there were local attacks in Hanover on Jews and synagogues.
- On 9th November, Hitler decided the attacks should go nationwide and ordered the police to not stop them. The attacks had to appear as if they were being carried out by ordinary German citizens, not the Nazi Party *(p.44)*.
- Gangs all over Germany attacked Jewish businesses, homes and synagogues.

## What were the results of Kristallnacht?

There were 4 key results of Kristallnacht:

- Approximately 200 synagogues were burned.
- About 100 Jews were murdered.
- 20,000 Jews were arrested and put in concentration camps by 12th November, 1938.
- The Nazis *(p.44)* fined the Jews 1 billion marks.

## What was the significance of Kristallnacht?

Kristallnacht was significant because it became the turning point in what was considered acceptable behaviour and attitudes toward the Jewish population. After this event, violence against Jews was now considered acceptable.

---

**DID YOU KNOW?**

Jewish people were considered by Nazis to be 'undesirable'.

# OPPOSITION TO THE NAZI REGIME

*Opposition to the Nazi government was difficult and dangerous.*

### Was there opposition to the Nazi regime?
There was some opposition to the Nazi *(p.44)* regime, but it was very limited because of the impact of the Nazi police state, propaganda, and censorship.

### Who opposed the Nazi government?
There were various groups that opposed the Nazi *(p.44)* regime. These included trade unions, the youth *(p.80)*, soldiers, priests, and other political groups.

### Why did people oppose the Nazi government?
Each group opposed the Nazi *(p.44)* regime for different reasons. For example, the churches opposed the Nazis and their policies because of their religious beliefs.

### How did people oppose the Nazi government?
There were 2 main ways in which people could oppose the Nazi *(p.44)* government.

- Passive opposition involved simply not following the rules imposed by the Nazis *(p.44)*. For example, young *(p.80)* people who opposed the Nazis listened and danced to banned music *(p.76)*. Members of secret trade union groups might call in sick and not work.
- Active opposition involved trying to disrupt or bring down the Nazi *(p.44)* regime. This included violent acts such as assassination attempts. This type of opposition was less common.

### How did the trade unions oppose the Nazi regime?
Although all independent trade unions had been made illegal, the Communist Party secretly encouraged workers to oppose the Nazi *(p.44)* government by faking sickness or disrupting production by committing acts of sabotage, for example breaking machines.

### How did the young oppose the Nazi regime?
The youth *(p.80)* opposition groups such as the Edelweiss Pirates or the Swing Youth *(p.95)* behaved in ways that went against Nazi *(p.44)* ideas. The Swing Youth listened to illegal American music *(p.76)*, wore American-style clothing, drank alcohol and smoked.

### How did the army oppose the Nazi regime?
Some army officers opposed the Nazi *(p.44)* regime. In 1938, a group led by General Ludwig Beck, chief of staff of the German Army, planned to assassinate Hitler. The plan was called off but they tried again in 1943 and 1944.

### How did the churches oppose the Nazi regime?
The Nazis *(p.44)* tried to control the churches in Germany but there was some opposition. About 6,000 Protestant pastors joined the Confessing Church, which opposed the Nazis. Some Catholic priests also spoke out against them.

### Why was opposition to the Nazi regime limited?
Opposition was limited because the Nazi *(p.44)* regime could easily arrest anyone who stood against it and send them to concentration camps, as happened to around 800 Protestant pastors.

> **DID YOU KNOW?**
>
> 3 facts about opposition to the Nazis:
> - ✓ Opposition was sometimes shown in small ways. For example, by not saying 'Sieg Heil.'
> - ✓ The Social Democrats printed their newspaper even though it had been made illegal by the Nazis.
> - ✓ Some Germans helped Jewish people by hiding them.

## SWING YOUTH

*Some members of the Swing Youth groups would say, 'Swing Heil!' instead of, 'Sieg Heil.'*

### Who were the Swing Youth?

The Swing Youth was a middle-class movement that started in many large German towns. They wanted to listen to jazz music *(p.76)*.

### Why were the Swing Youth not allowed to listen to jazz music?

The Nazis *(p.44)* considered jazz music *(p.76)* 'degenerate' because of its links to African Americans.

### What happened to the Swing Youth?

The Nazis *(p.44)* were threatened by Swing Youth's activities so closed down the bars they were known to attend. Some members of the movement were arrested and given short sentences in concentration camps.

> **DID YOU KNOW?**
>
> The Swing Youth movement started in 1939.

## EDELWEISS PIRATES

*The Edelweiss Pirates focused on rebelling against what the Nazis expected of the young.*

### Who were the Edelweiss Pirates?

The Edelweiss Pirates were a working class movement that started in 1937. They hated the Hitler Youth *(p.80)*.

### What did the Edelweiss Pirates do?

They would beat up Hitler Youth *(p.80)* members. They also wore clothing unacceptable to the Nazis *(p.44)* and listened to music *(p.76)* that was banned.

### What impact did the Edelweiss Pirates have?
While they were never a real threat to the Nazis *(p.44)*, their activities increased as the war progressed. They provided shelter for army deserters and helped prisoners escape from concentration camps. They derailed trains going to the camps and stole food and supplies.

> **DID YOU KNOW?**
>
> **3 facts about the Edelweiss Pirates.**
> - ✔ Edelweiss is a white flower that grows in the Alps.
> - ✔ The Nazis saw the group as more of threat during the Second World War.
> - ✔ Some members were executed in 1944 for their activities.

# WHITE ROSE GROUP
*The White Rose group were the most famous youth opposition group.*

### Who were the White Rose Group?
The White Rose Group was started by students Hans and Sophie Scholl and Professor Kurt Huber at Munich University.

### What did the White Rose Group do?
They criticised the continuation of the war and the treatment of Jews and Slavs and between 1942 and 1943, they published anti-Nazi leaflets and wrote graffiti on buildings in Munich.

### What happened to the White Rose Group?
In February 1943, Sophie and Hans Scholl were reported for distributing leaflets at Munich University to the Gestapo *(p.66)*. They were both arrested, found guilty of treason and executed on 4th February, 1943.

> **DID YOU KNOW?**
>
> The White Rose group believed in non-violent resistance to the Nazis.

# CHARLES G DAWES
*Charles G. Dawes received the Nobel Peace Prize in 1925, for reducing tension between Germany and France.*

### Who was Charles G Dawes?
Charles G Dawes was an American banker who was asked by the Allies to help solve the problem of Weimar Germany not being able to pay its reparations bill.

### When was Charles G Dawes important?
Charles G Dawes was important in 1924.

### Why was Charles G Dawes important to the Weimar Republic?
Charles G Dawes was important because he negotiated the Dawes Plan *(p.32)* with Gustav Stresemann *(p.109)*. This plan helped Weimar Germany end the hyperinflation crisis, stabilise the currency and organise American loans to Weimar Germany to support their economy.

> **DID YOU KNOW?**
>
> Charles G Dawes was the vice president of the US, between 1925 and 1929.
>
> He was a member of the Republican Party.

# ANTON DREXLER
*Anton Drexler wanted the DAP to be a party for the workers and anti-capitalist.*

### Who was Anton Drexler?
Anton Drexler was a German locksmith who created the German Workers' Party (DAP *(p.42)*), a right-wing nationalist political party.

### When was Anton Drexler important?
Anton Drexler was important from 1919 to 1921.

### Why was Anton Drexler important to the Weimar Republic?
Anton Drexler was important due to 3 key reasons:

- ✓ He set up the German Workers' Party (DAP *(p.42)*) which eventually became the Nazi Party *(p.44)*. The DAP was a right-wing nationalist party that was anti-Semitic and despised the Treaty of Versailles.
- ✓ With Hitler, he wrote the Twenty-Five Point Programme in January 1920, which outlined the party's policies.
- ✓ He was replaced by Hitler as the leader of the Nazi Party *(p.44)* (NSDAP) in July 1921.

> **DID YOU KNOW?**
>
> **3 facts about Anton Drexler:**
> - ✓ He did not play a major role in the Nazi Party after the Munich Beer Hall Putsch.
> - ✓ He died in Munich in 1942.
> - ✓ He had a strained relationship with Hitler after he took over the party.

# FRIEDRICH EBERT

*'Without democracy there is no freedom. Violence, no matter who is using it, is always reactionary.'*
*Friedrich Ebert in 1919.*

### Who was Friedrich Ebert?

Friedrich Ebert was the leader of the Social Democratic Party (SPD) in Germany and involved with the creation of the Weimar Republic *(p. 18)*.

### When was Friedrich Ebert in power?

Ebert became the last chancellor of the kaiser's government on 9th November, 1918. After the war, he became the first president of the Weimar Republic *(p. 18)* in February 1919 and held office until February 1925.

### Why was Friedrich Ebert important?

Ebert was important for 5 main reasons:

- He helped Germany change from a monarchy under Kaiser Wilhelm II to the Weimar Republic *(p. 18)*, a democracy.
- He helped create the new constitution.
- He was one of the politicians who signed the Treaty of Versailles and became known as one of the 'November Criminals'.
- He worked with the kaiser's civil servants to keep the country running as the country changed from a monarchy to a republic.
- He did a deal with General Groener so that he and the army would work together to stop the communists from taking power.

> **DID YOU KNOW?**
>
> Friedrich Ebert learnt his father's trade and was a saddle maker before he became a politician.

# JOSEPH GOEBBELS

*'The point of a political speech is to persuade people of what we think right. I speak differently in the provinces than I do in Berlin, and when I speak in Bayreuth, I say different things than I say in the Pharus Hall.' Joseph Goebbels in 1928.*

### Who was Joseph Goebbels?

Joseph Goebbels tried to develop a career in journalism and writing novels and plays. He joined the Nazi Party *(p. 44)* and became one of its leading officials.

### When was Joseph Goebbels important?

Joseph Goebbels was important between 1924, when he joined the Nazi Party *(p. 44)*, and 1945 when he committed suicide.

### What was Joseph Goebbels famous for?

Joseph Goebbels had 4 key roles in the Nazi Party *(p. 44)*:

- He became the party leader in Berlin in 1926.

- He became a member of the Reichstag in 1928.
- He was put in charge of propaganda for the Nazi Party (p.44) in 1928.
- He was made the minister of people's enlightenment and propaganda in March 1933.

### When did Joseph Goebbels die?

Joseph Goebbels committed suicide on 1st May, 1945.

> **DID YOU KNOW?**
>
> Joseph Goebbels did not fit the idea of a 'Aryan'
> - He walked with a limp due to a clubfoot.
> - The German Army rejected him when he tried to join during the First World War.
> - He was about five feet tall.

# RUDOLF HESS

*Rudolf Hess was given a life sentence at the Nuremberg Trials, which he served at Spandau Prison until he died in 1987.*

### Who was Rudolf Hess?

Rudolf Hess was a wealthy academic who had fought in the German Army during the First World War and trained as a pilot in 1918. He later became Hitler's right hand man and deputy Führer.

### When was Rudolf Hess important?

Rudolf Hess was important between 1920 and 1941.

### What role did Rudolf Hess play in the Nazi Party?

Rudolf Hess was important because of 3 key reasons:
- He joined the NSDAP (p.44) in 1920 and became Hitler's deputy in 1933.
- He took part in the Nazi Party's (p.44) failed Munich Beer Hall Putsch (p.46) in 1923.
- He betrayed Hitler when he flew to Britain in 1941 to ask for peace. He was arrested and treated as a prisoner of war.

> **DID YOU KNOW?**
>
> Hess flew to Scotland in 1941 in an attempt to negotiate peace.

# REINHARD HEYDRICH
*Reinhard Heydrich was assassinated by Czechoslovak agents in 1942.*

### Who was Reinhard Heydrich?
Reinhard Heydrich was a naval officer between 1922 and 1931. He was a leading Nazi *(p.44)* official.

### When was Reinhard Heydrich important?
Reinhard Heydrich was important between 1931 and 1942.

### Why was Reinhard Heydrich important in Nazi Germany?
Reinhard Heydrich was an important figure in the Nazi Party *(p.44)* holding 4 key roles under the regime:

- He joined the SS *(p.65)* in August 1931.
- He became the leader of the Security Service (Sicherheitsdienst; SD *(p.66)*).
- In April 1933, he was made the deputy-leader, under Himmler, of the Gestapo *(p.66)*, or secret police. In 1934 he became the leader of the Gestapo.
- In September 1939, Heydrich became the leader of a new organisation called the Reich Security Main Office (Reichssicherheitshauptamt or RSHA). This was created by merging the Gestapo *(p.66)* and SD *(p.66)*.

> **DID YOU KNOW?**
>
> **The assassination of Reinhard Heydrich led to reprisals by the Nazis.**
> There were mass arrests and executions in Czechoslovakia where Heydrich was murdered.

# HEINRICH HIMMLER
*'The best political weapon is the weapon of terror. Cruelty commands respect. Men may hate us. But, we don't ask for their love; only for their fear.' Heinrich Himmler.*

### Who was Heinrich Himmler?
Heinrich Himmler was a soldier in the German Army during the First World War and had several jobs after the war, including raising chickens. He joined the Nazi Party *(p.44)* and was one of the party's leading officials.

### When was Heinrich Himmler important?
Heinrich Himmler was important from 1925, when he joined the Nazi Party *(p.44)*, until 1945 when he committed suicide.

### What role did Heinrich Himmler play in the Nazi Party?
Heinrich Himmler had 4 main roles in the Nazi Party *(p.44)*:

- He was appointed head of the SS *(p.65)*, Schutzstaffel or 'Blackshirts' in 1929.
- He became head of the Munich police, the commander of all German police and set up the first concentration camp *(p.67)* at Dachau in 1933.
- He was appointed the minister for the interior in 1943.
- He played a major role in the 'Final Solution', the mass murder of all Jews in Europe.

### When did Heinrich Himmler die?
Heinrich Himmler committed suicide on 23rd May, 1945.

> **DID YOU KNOW?**
>
> Heinrich Himmler had been a chicken farmer after the First World War.

# PRESIDENT PAUL VON HINDENBURG
*President von Hindenburg showed great contempt for Hitler and calling him 'that Bohemian corporal.'*

### Who was Field Marshal Paul von Hindenburg?
Field Marshal Paul von Hindenburg was an important German military figure in the First World War and was elected the second president of the Weimar Republic *(p.18)*.

### When was Field Marshal Hindenburg important?
Field Marshal Paul von Hindenburg was important from 1914 to 1934.

### What was role of Field Marshal Hindenburg in the First World War?
Field Marshal Hindenburg had 4 key roles during the First World War:
- Field Marshal Hindenburg commanded the German armies on the Eastern Front with his friend and second in command, General Ludendorff.
- By the end of the war, he commanded the entire Imperial German Army and those of the other Central Powers.
- He ruled Germany as part of a military dictatorship until October 1918.
- It was Hindenburg who told the kaiser that the German Army would not continue to fight in October 1918.

### What was significance of Field Marshal Hindenburg in the Weimar Republic?
Paul von Hindenburg played a significant role in the Weimar Republic *(p.18)* for 6 key reasons:
- He became the commander of the Germany army in 1916 and was in charge when Germany surrendered in November 1918. He allowed General von Ludendorff to take the blame for the defeat.
- He was elected president of the Weimar Republic *(p.18)* in April 1925.
- Hitler opposed him in the presidential elections in March and April 1932 and lost.
- Hindenburg is best known for attempting to block Hitler from becoming the chancellor of Weimar Germany.
- However, he was persuaded by Franz von Papen to appoint Hitler as chancellor on 30th January, 1933 and thus aided the collapse of the Weimar Republic *(p.18)*.
- His death in 1934 was a key event in Hitler's creation of a dictatorship as Hitler merged the role of chancellor and president into one: the Führer.

### When did Paul von Hindenburg die?
President Paul von Hindenburg died on 2nd August, 1934.

> **DID YOU KNOW?**
>
> Towards the end of his his life, President von Hindenburg showed signs of senility.

# ADOLF HITLER

*Adolf Hitler said, 'I want to call to account the November Criminals of 1918. It cannot be that two million Germans have fallen in vain. We demand revenge.'*

### Who was Hitler?

Adolf Hitler was the leader of the Nazi Party *(p.44)*. In 1933 he became the chancellor of Germany. He was called the Führer from 1934 onwards. During his dictatorship - which ran between 1933 and 1945 - he started the Second World War.

### When was Hitler born?

Hitler was born in Austria, in April 1889.

### What was Hitler's early life like?

There were 5 main events in Hitler's early life:

- Hitler had a turbulent upbringing and was beaten by his father. He was very close to his mother and was heavily traumatised when she died when he was just 18 years old.
- Hitler's early life saw him attempt a career as an artist - however he was rejected from art school in Vienna and became homeless for several years.
- During the First World War, he won the Iron Cross for bravery while delivering an important message on the front line.
- Hitler hated that Germany lost the war and later came to despise the Treaty of Versailles and the politicians who signed it.
- He hated the new Weimar government and joined the little known German Workers' Party in 1919.

### When was Hitler in power?

Hitler was appointed chancellor of Germany by President Paul von Hindenburg *(p.101)* on 30th January, 1933. He became the Führer - a German word meaning leader - in 1934.

### What happened to Hitler at the Munich Putsch?

The Munich Putsch *(p.46)*, also known as the Beer Hall Putsch was a failed armed rebellion by the Nazi Party *(p.44)* between the 8th and 9th November, 1923. Hitler wanted to overthrow the Weimar Republic *(p.18)* and become Germany's president.

### What did Hitler do in prison?

In prison Hitler wrote 'Mein Kampf', his autobiography, which outlined his political beliefs.

### What did Hitler's book, 'Mein Kampf', state?

'Mein Kampf' contained 4 key ideas:

- ✅ Democracy should be destroyed.
- ✅ The cancellation of the Treaty of the Versailles, which he hated.
- ✅ German territories should be expanded.
- ✅ His perceived inferiority of the Jews.

## What was Hitler's personality like?

Hitler's public persona included the following:

- ✅ Presenting himself as a strong, organised leader.
- ✅ He was a mesmerising public speaker.
- ✅ Presenting himself as someone who understood Germany's troubles and offered the solutions, including dealing with the betrayal many Germans felt when the First World War ended.

## Why was Hitler prejudiced?

Hitler held prejudiced views against several groups of people. The following reasons likely explain why:

- ✅ At the time Hitler was growing up, it was very common to encounter anti-Semitic beliefs. He certainly would have been aware of these ideas from a young *(p.80)* age.
- ✅ The family doctor who revealed to Hitler that his mother was dying of cancer had been Jewish.
- ✅ When living homeless in Vienna he would have encountered many groups of people, who were at the time more successful than himself.
- ✅ Following Germany's defeat in the war, the Armistice and Treaty of Versailles were signed by some Jewish politicians.
- ✅ Hitler certainly had very strong anti-Semitic beliefs by the time he wrote 'Mein Kampf' in 1924, and it was clear he was using Jews as a scapegoat for Germany's problems.

## How did Hitler became Führer?

There were several key steps in Hitler's path to Führer. The final step was the death of President Hindenburg *(p.101)* on 2nd August, 1934. Hitler merged his role of chancellor with that of president, making himself the new Führer.

## How did Hitler expect to be shown loyalty?

There were 3 main ways people showed loyalty to Hitler.

- ✅ People demonstrated their loyalty through the 'Heil Hitler' salute.
- ✅ From 20th August, 1934, the army was forced to swear an oath of allegiance to him personally, rather than to Germany,
- ✅ School children in Germany recited the morning pledge in school, promising 'to fight, obey and die' for their Führer.

## How did Hitler run Germany?

Under Hitler, Germany became a police state. This meant every aspect of daily life for German citizens was controlled by the police. It was a ruthless regime.

---

**DID YOU KNOW?**

**3 facts about Hitler:**
- ✓ Hitler was born in Austria.
- ✓ He moved to Vienna and applied to several art schools.
- ✓ He was rejected from the art schools, was homeless for a while and sold postcards he had painted to tourists.

# DR WOLFGANG KAPP

*Dr Kapp was a lawyer and politician who campaigned for the return of the Kaiser in the 1920s.*

### Who was Wolfgang Kapp?
Dr Wolfgang Kapp was a right-wing nationalist who disliked the Weimar Republic *(p.18)*.

### What did Wolfgang Kapp do?
Dr Wolfgang Kapp is famous for leading a right-wing uprising of the Freikorps against the Weimar Republic *(p.18)* in March 1920. It failed because the workers went on strike.

### Was Dr Wolfgang Kapp punished?
Dr Wolfgang Kapp fled to Sweden. He returned to Germany, and while he was waiting to be put on trial, he died of cancer.

---

**DID YOU KNOW?**

**3 facts about Kapp:**
- ✓ Kapp was born in New York.
- ✓ He was a nationalist.
- ✓ He founded the German Fatherland Party.

---

# KARL LIEBKNECHT

*Karl Liebknecht played an important role in the Spartacist Uprising.*

### Who was Karl Liebknecht?
Karl Liebknecht was one of the leaders of the Spartacist League who were a group of extreme socialists from the Independent Socialist Party (USPD) and supporters of the Communist Party in Germany.

### When was Karl Liebknecht active?
Karl Liebknecht led the Spartacist uprising *(p.27)* in January 1919.

### Why was Karl Liebknecht important to the Weimar Republic?
Karl Liebknecht was important because he and Rosa Luxemburg led a failed attempt to overthrow the Weimar Republic *(p.18)* in January 1919.

### When did Karl Liebknecht die?
Karl Liebknecht died on 16th January, 1919.

### Who killed Karl Liebknecht?
Karl Liebknecht was killed by members of the Freikorps.

> **DID YOU KNOW?**
>
> **3 facts about Karl Liebknecht:**
> - ✓ There is a memorial to him in the Tiergarten, Berlin.
> - ✓ He was very anti-militarism. He was the only member of the Reichstag who voted against Germany's entry into the First World War.
> - ✓ He was arrested because of his political activities.

# GENERAL LUDENDORFF

*General Ludendorff was a General in the First World War and took part in the Munich Beer Hall Putsch.*

### Who was General von Ludendorff?

General von Ludendorff was considered one of Germany's greatest generals of the First World War. He was seen as a hero for his efforts on both the Eastern and Western Fronts. He became involved with the Nazi Party's *(p.44)* failed Munich Beer Hall Putsch *(p.46)* in 1923.

### When was General Ludendorff important?

General von Ludendorff was important between the years 1914 and 1923.

### Why was General von Ludendorff important to the Weimar Republic?

General von Ludendorff was important during the Weimar Republic *(p.18)* for 5 main reasons:

- ☑ He led the massive German offensive against the Allies in March 1918 called the 'Ludendorff Offensive' which failed.
- ☑ He created the stab-in-the-back myth to cover for his own failings during the war and place the blame on democratic politicians who led the Weimar Republic *(p.18)* after the war.
- ☑ He supported Dr Wolfgang Kapp in the Kapp Putsch *(p.28)* in March 1920.
- ☑ He took part in the Nazi Party's *(p.44)* failed Beer Hall Putsch *(p.46)* in November 1923.
- ☑ He was put on trial because of his role in the Munich Beer Hall Putsch *(p.46)* but was found not guilty.

> **DID YOU KNOW?**
>
> General Ludendorff planned the Ludendorff Offensive of the First World War. After it failed, he resigned and fled to Sweden at the end of the war.

## ROSA LUXEMBURG

*Rosa Luxemburg said, 'Freedom is the freedom of those who think differently.'*

### Who was Rosa Luxemburg?
Rosa Luxemburg was one of the leaders of the Spartacist League who were a group of extreme socialists from the Independent Socialist Party (USPD) and supporters of the Communist Party in Germany.

### When was Rosa Luxemburg active?
Rosa Luxemburg led the Spartacist uprising *(p.27)* in January 1919.

### What was Rosa Luxemburg important to the Weimar Republic?
Rosa Luxemburg was important because she and Karl Liebknecht led a failed attempt to overthrow the Weimar Republic *(p.18)* in January 1919.

### When did Rosa Luxemburg die?
Rosa Luxemburg died on 16th January, 1919.

### Who killed Rosa Luxemburg?
Rosa Luxemburg was killed by members of the Freikorps and her body was dumped in a canal in Berlin.

---

**DID YOU KNOW?**

**3 facts about Rosa Luxemburg:**
- ✓ She was born in the Russian Empire.
- ✓ She was arrested quite a few times because of her political activities.
- ✓ She wrote several books.

---

## FRANZ VON PAPEN

*Franz von Papen was put on trial at Nuremberg and found not guilty of contributing to the start of the Second World War.*

### Who was Franz von Papen?
Franz von Papen was a member of the Catholic Centre Party or Zentrum Partei in the Weimar Republic *(p.18)*. He was inadvertently instrumental in the collapse of the Weimar Republic and allowing Hitler to seize power.

### When was Franz von Papen important?
Franz von Papen was important between 1932 and 1933.

### What was important about Franz von Papen?
Franz von Papen was important because of 4 key events:
- ☑ He became chancellor of the Weimar Republic *(p.18)* when General von Schleicher *(p.108)* persuaded President von Hindenburg *(p.101)* to appoint him in May 1932.

- He could not get the support of the Reichstag to pass his laws.
- General von Schleicher *(p.108)* persuaded the president to sack von Papen as chancellor and appoint himself instead.
- He worked with Hitler to undermine Chancellor von Schleicher. He persuaded the president to sack von Schleicher and appoint Hitler as chancellor on 30th January, 1933.

> **DID YOU KNOW?**
>
> Von Papen was vice chancellor under Hitler from 1933 to 1934.

# ERNST RÖHM

*'Hitler can't walk over me as he might have done a year ago; I've seen to that. Don't forget that I have three million men, with every key position in the hands of my own people, Hitler knows that I have friends in the Reichswehr, you know!' Ernst Röhm in 1934.*

## Who was Ernst Röhm?

Ernst Röhm was an ex-soldier who fought in the German Army during the First World War. He joined the German Workers' Party (DAP *(p.42)*), which became the Nazi Party *(p.44)*. He was one their top officials and the leader of the SA *(p.43)*.

## When was Ernst Röhm important?

Ernst Röhm was important from when he joined the party in 1919 until he was assassinated during the Night of the Long Knives in 1934.

## What role did Ernst Röhm play in the Nazi Party?

Ernst Röhm had played 3 key roles in the Nazi Party *(p.44)*:

- He became the leader of the SA *(p.43)* - the Sturmabteilung or the 'Brownshirts' - in 1921.
- He took part in the Nazi Party's *(p.44)* failed Munich Beer Hall Putsch *(p.46)*, 1923.
- He was assassinated by members of the SS *(p.65)* during the Night of the Long Knives, June 1934.

## Why was Ernst Röhm assassinated?

There were 4 main reasons why Ernst Röhm was assassinated by members of the SS *(p.65)* during the Night of the Long Knives:

- He was a threat to Hitler's position as the leader of the Nazi Party *(p.44)* because the 3 million members of the SA *(p.43)* were loyal to Röhm.
- He disagreed with Hitler about some of the Nazi Party's *(p.44)* policies. Röhm wanted to focus more on the workers and criticised Hitler's close relationship with big business.
- He wanted to merge the German Army with the SA *(p.43)*. This alarmed Hitler and the army.
- Hitler wanted to ensure that the leaders of the German Army were happy as they had the power to overthrow him.

## When did Ernst Röhm die?

Ernst Röhm was shot dead on 1st July, 1934.

> **DID YOU KNOW?**
>
> David Low, a cartoonist, drew a very famous cartoon after the Night of the Long Knives in 1934.
>
> The cartoon is called, 'They salute with both hands now!' This is a reference to the Nazi salute, only in David Low's cartoon it shows the SA saluting with both hands. They have their hands up in surrender after the murder of Ernst Röhm and others.

# PHILIPP SCHEIDEMANN

*Philipp Scheidemann fled to Denmark when Hitler became chancellor in 1933.*

## Who was Philipp Scheidemann?

Philipp Scheidemann was a leading member of the Social Democratic Party in Germany.

## Why was Philipp Scheidemann important?

Scheidemann announced there was a new German Republic from a window of the Reichstag after he heard that Kaiser Wilhelm II had abdicated on 9th November, 1918.

> **DID YOU KNOW?**
>
> **3 facts about Philipp Scheidemann:**
> - ✓ He was the Weimar Republic's first president.
> - ✓ He resigned because he disagreed with the Treaty of Versailles.
> - ✓ There was an assassination attempt on his life in 1922.

# GENERAL VON SCHLEICHER

*General von Schleicher and his wife were assassinated by the SS during the Night of the Long Knives.*

## Who was General von Schleicher?

General Kurt von Schleicher was a general in the Germany army during the First World War. He was involved with the political deals that helped Hitler become chancellor *(p.56)* on 30th January, 1933.

## When was General von Schleicher important?

General Kurt von Schleicher was important in Weimar Germany between 1932 and 1933.

## What was important about General von Schleicher?

General Kurt von Schleicher was important for 4 main reasons:

- He persuaded President von Hindenburg *(p.101)* to sack Chancellor Brüning in May 1932 and appoint Franz von Papen instead.
- He persuaded President von Hindenburg *(p.101)* to sack Chancellor von Papen in November 1932 and appoint himself as chancellor in December instead.
- This led to von Papen and Hitler plotting against him. As a result, President von Hindenburg *(p.101)* sacked him as chancellor and appointed Hitler on 30th January, 1933.
- He was assassinated during the Night of the Long Knives on 30th June, 1934.

### When did General von Schleicher die?
General Kurt von Schleicher was assassinated on 30th June, 1934.

> **DID YOU KNOW?**
> Von Schleicher fought in the First World War.

# GUSTAV STRESEMANN
*Gustav Stresemann was foreign minister of Germany from 1923 to 1929.*

### Who was Gustav Stresemann?
Gustav Stresemann was a German statesman who served as chancellor and foreign minister for the Weimar Republic *(p.18)*.

### When was Gustav Stresemann in power?
Stresemann had multiple roles in Germany:
- In 1907, he became a member of Germany's parliament.
- In 1917, he became the leader of the National Liberal Party.
- In 1923, he was the chancellor between August and November.
- From August 1923, he also became foreign secretary.

### Why was Gustav Stresemann important?
Stresemann was important because:
- He stopped the hyperinflation crisis of 1923.
- He was a better politician than Ebert and also held more right-wing support, which resulted in less hostility towards the Weimar Republic *(p.18)*.
- His actions helped the Weimar Republic *(p.18)* to recover between 1924 and 1929.
- He helped create the Dawes Plan *(p.32)* in 1924 which led to a temporary reduction in the annual reparation payments and American loans to German businesses and banks.
- He helped restore Germany's confidence and reputation so that Germany's relationship with other countries improved.
- Germany was allowed to join the League of Nations under his leadership.
- Right-wing Germans criticised him for not demanding back some of the land taken away in the Treaty of Versailles and not ending reparations.

### How did Gustav Stresemann stop hyperinflation?

Stresemann solved the hyperinflation crisis by:

- Firstly, he called off the passive strike in the Ruhr as this was further damaging the economy.
- He then called for the old currency to be recalled and destroyed.
- He set up a temporary currency called the Rentenmark, which had real value and was important in halting hyperinflation.
- He negotiated the Dawes Plan *(p.32)* in 1924.
- Lastly, in 1924, he replaced the Rentenmark with a new currency, the Reichsmark, which was tied to the price of land in Germany.

> **DID YOU KNOW?**
>
> Stresemann died of a stroke in 1929.

# KAISER WILHELM II

*Kaiser Wilhelm II was born with a deformed left arm.*

### Who was Kaiser Wilhelm II?

Kaiser Wilhelm II was the emperor, or king, of Germany during the First World War.

### When was Kaiser Wilhelm II in power?

Kaiser Wilhelm II was the ruler of Germany between 1888 and 1918.

### What happened to the Kaiser Wilhelm II at the end of the First World War?

Kaiser Wilhelm II was the last emperor of Germany and forced to abdicate on 9th November 1918, as requested in the peace agreement from the Allies.

> **DID YOU KNOW?**
>
> **Kaiser Wilhelm II's foreign policy was not very successful after Bismarck, his chancellor, resigned in 1890. Bismarck did not get on with the new kaiser.**
>
> Bismarck said, 'The kaiser is like a balloon: if you don't keep fast hold of the string, you never know where he will be off to.'

# OWEN YOUNG

*Owen Young trained as a lawyer. When he retired he returned to his roots and became a dairy farmer.*

### Who was Owen Young?

Owen Young was an American banker who was asked by the Allies to help resolve the reparations issues with Weimar Germany.

### When was Owen Young important?

Owen Young was important in 1929.

### What was Owen Young's role in the Weimar Republic?

Owen Young was important because he helped negotiate the Young Plan *(p.36)* with Stresemann. This plan reduced the overall reparation bill that Weimar Germany had to pay from £6.6 billion to £2 billion and gave the country 59 more years to pay it.

**DID YOU KNOW?**

Young was a member of the German Reparations International Commission.

# GLOSSARY

## A

Abdicate - to give up a position of power or a responsibility.

Abolish, Abolished - to stop something, or get rid of it.

Abolition - the act of abolishing something, i.e. to stop or get rid of it.

Agriculture - an umbrella term to do with farming, growing crops or raising animals.

Allegiance - loyalty to a person, group or cause.

Allies - parties working together for a common objective, such as countries involved in a war. In both world wars, 'Allies' refers to those countries on the side of Great Britain.

Anti-Semitic - to be against, or hostile to, Jews.

Armistice - an agreement between two or more opposing sides in a war to stop fighting.

Arson - the act of deliberately starting a fire.

Artillery - large guns used in warfare.

Aryan - a member of the 'master race' perceived by the Nazis, who had the idea of a pure German race.

Assassinate - to murder someone, usually an important figure, often for religious or political reasons.

Assassination - the act of murdering someone, usually an important person.

Authoritarian - either a person who believes in strict obedience to those in authority or a system of government in which there are few freedoms.

Autobahn - the German motorway system.

## B

Bankrupt - to be insolvent; to have run out of resources with which to pay existing debts.

Boycott - a way of protesting or bringing about change by refusing to buy something or use services.

## C

Cabinet - politically, the group of senior ministers responsible for controlling government policy.

Campaign - a political movement to get something changed; in military terms, it refers to a series of operations to achieve a goal.

Capitalism - the idea of goods and services being exchanged for money, private ownership of property and businesses, and acceptance of a hierarchical society.

Castrated - referring to a man whose testicles have been removed to prevent reproduction.

Casualties - people who have been injured or killed, such as during a war, accident or catastrophe.

Catholic - a Christian who belongs to the Roman Catholic Church.

Ceasefire - when the various sides involved in conflict agree to stop fighting.

Censorship - the control of information in the media by a government, whereby information considered obscene or unacceptable is suppressed.

Chancellor - a senior state official who, in some countries, is the head of the government and responsible for the day-to-day running of the nation.

Civil liberties - the set of basic freedoms citizens expect in a democracy, such as freedom of speech or freedom of religion.

Civil rights - the rights a citizen has to political or social freedoms, such as the right to vote or freedom of speech.

Civil servant - a person who works for the government, either at national or local level.

Civilian - a non-military person.

Claim - someone's assertion of their right to something - for example, a claim to the throne.

Coalition government - a government formed by more than one political party.

Colonies, Colony - a country or area controlled by another country and occupied by settlers.

Communism - the belief, based on the ideas of Karl Marx, that all people should be equal in society without government, money or private property. Everything is owned by by the people, and each person receives according to need.

Communist - a believer in communism.

Concentration camp - a place where large numbers of people are imprisoned with inadequate facilities. Conditions are harsh and they are forced to work or kept there to await execution. The term is most frequently used in connection with the Nazis.

Concordat - a treaty signed in July 1933 between the Catholic Church and the Nazis that effectively meant they would stay out of each others' affairs.

Conference - a formal meeting to discuss common issues of interest or concern.

Conscription - mandatory enlistment of people into a state service, usually the military.

Conservative - someone who dislikes change and prefers traditional values. It can also refer to a member of the Conservative Party.

Consolidate - to strengthen a position, often politically, by bringing several things together into a more effective whole.

Constitution - rules, laws or principles that set out how a country is governed.

Constitutional assembly - group of elected representatives gathered specifically to draft a new constitution for a country.

Consumer goods - products that people buy.

Cooperate, Cooperation - to work together to achieve a common aim. Frequently used in relation to politics, economics or law.

# GLOSSARY

**Corrupt** - when someone is willing to act dishonestly for their own personal gain.

**Coup** - a sudden, violent and illegal overthrow of the government by a small group - for example, the chiefs of an army.

**Currency** - an umbrella term for any form of legal tender, but most commonly referring to money.

## D

**Death camp** - another name for an extermination camp in Nazi Germany.

**Debt** - when something, usually money, is owed by a person, organisation or institution to another.

**Decree** - an official order with the force of law behind it.

**Demilitarised** - to remove all military forces from an area and forbid them to be stationed there.

**Democracy** - a political system where a population votes for its government on a regular basis. The word is Greek for 'the rule of people' or 'people power'.

**Democratic** - relating to or supporting the principles of democracy.

**Deport** - to expel someone from a country and, usually, return them to their homeland.

**Dictator** - a ruler with absolute power over a country, often acquired by force.

**Dictatorship** - a form of government where an individual or small group has total power, ruling without tolerance for other views or opposition.

**Diktat** - a penalty or settlement imposed on a defeated party. The Germans called the Treaty of Versailles a 'diktat', or 'dictated peace'.

**Dispute** - a disagreement or argument; often used to describe conflict between different countries.

## E

**Economic** - relating to the economy; also used when justifying something in terms of profitability.

**Economic depression** - a sustained downturn in the economy.

**Economy** - a country, state or region's position in terms of production and consumption of goods and services, and the supply of money.

**Electorate** - a group of people who are eligible to vote.

**Embassy** - historically, a deputation sent by one ruler, state or country to another. More recently, it is also the accepted name for the official residence or offices of an ambassador.

**Empire** - a group of states or countries ruled over and controlled by a single monarch.

**Exile** - to be banned from one's original country, usually as a punishment or for political reasons.

**Extreme** - furthest from the centre or any given point. If someone holds extreme views, they are not moderate and are considered radical.

## F

**Fascism** - an extreme right-wing belief system based around racism and national pride. It was created by the Italian dictator, Benito Mussolini, and later adopted by Adolf Hitler.

**Fascist** - one who believes in fascism.

**Fixed income** - a regular, set amount of money received by someone, such as a salary or pension, which does not change.

**Foreign policy** - a government's strategy for dealing with other nations.

## G

**Ghetto** - part of a city, often a slum area, occupied by a minority group.

## H

**Hyperinflation** - rapid acceleration of inflation which typically sees a currency lose its value and become worthless. As a result, the price of goods skyrockets for a short period of time.

## I

**Ideology** - a set of ideas and ideals, particularly around political ideas or economic policy, often shared by a group of people.

**Imperial, Imperialisation, Imperialism, Imperialist** - is the practice or policy of taking possession of, and extending political and economic control over other areas or territories. Imperialism always requires the use of military, political or economic power by a stronger nation over that of a weaker one. An imperialist is someone who supports or practices imperialism and imperial relates to a system of empire, for example the British Empire.

**Import** - to bring goods or services into a different country to sell.

**Independence, Independent** - to be free of control, often meaning by another country, allowing the people of a nation the ability to govern themselves.

**Indoctrinate, Indoctrination** - to teach someone to accept a set of beliefs without reservation or question.

**Industrial** - related to industry, manufacturing and/or production.

**Industry** - the part of the economy concerned with turning raw materials into into manufactured goods, for example making furniture from wood.

**Inferior** - lower in rank, status or quality.

**Inflation** - the general increase in the prices of goods which means money does not buy as much as it used to.

**Informant** - someone who passes important information to another person or organisation, such as the police.

**Interim** - in the meantime; during an intervening period.

**Investor** - someone who puts money into something with the

## GLOSSARY

expectation of future profit.

Invisible unemployment - unemployment that is hidden because it is not counted in a government's official figures. For example, only those who are jobless but actively seeking work may be included.

### J

Juries, Jury - a group of people sworn to listen to evidence on a legal case and then deliver an impartial verdict based on what they have heard.

### K

Kaiser - the German word for a king or emperor.

### L

Left wing - used to describe political groups or individuals with beliefs that are usually centered around socialism and the idea of reform.

Legislation - a term for laws when they are considered collectively, for example housing legislation.

### M

Mandate - authority to carry out a policy.

Merchant, Merchants - someone who sells goods or services.

Middle class - refers to the socio-economic group which includes people who are educated and have professional jobs, such as teachers or lawyers.

Military force - the use of armed forces.

Minister - a senior member of government, usually responsible for a particular area such as education or finance.

Moderate - someone who is not extreme.

Modernise - to update something to make it suitable for modern times, often by using modern equipment or modern ideas.

Monarchy - a form of government in which the head of state is a monarch, a king or queen.

Mutiny - a rebellion or revolt, in particular by soldiers or sailors against their commanding officers.

### N

Nationalism, Nationalist, Nationalistic - identifying with your own nation and supporting its interests, often to the detriment or exclusion of other nations.

Negative Cohesion - Where someone focuses on negative aspects to unite people in their dislike of something.

### O

Oath - a solemn promise with special significance, often relating to future behaviour or actions.

Occupation - the action, state or period when somewhere is taken over and occupied by a military force.

Offensive - another way of saying an attack or campaign.

### P

POW, Prisoner of war, Prisoners of war - somebody who has been captured and taken prisoner by enemy forces.

Paramilitary - a group of unofficial or private soldiers organised along military lines.

Parliament - a group of politicians who make the laws of their country, usually elected by the population.

Passive resistance - to resist something without using violence but by not cooperating.

Persecute - to treat someone unfairly because of their race, religion or political beliefs.

Persecution - hostility towards or harassment of someone, usually due to their race, religion or political beliefs.

Plebiscite - a vote or referendum on an important matter in an area or country.

Police state - a totalitarian country in which the police have a great deal of power to control the people and suppress opposition.

Pope - the head of the Roman Catholic Church.

Population - the number of people who live in a specified place.

Poverty - the state of being extremely poor.

President - the elected head of state of a republic.

Production - a term used to describe how much of something is made, for example saying a factory has a high production rate.

Profit - generally refers to financial gain; the amount of money made after deducting buying, operating or production costs.

Propaganda - biased information aimed at persuading people to think a certain way.

Proportional representation - a system of voting in which political parties gain seats in proportion to the number of votes they receive in an election.

Prosecute - to institute or conduct legal proceedings against a person or organisation.

Prosperity - the state of thriving, enjoying good fortune and/or social status.

Protestant - someone belonging to the branch of the Christian Church that separated from the Roman Catholic Church in the 16th century.

Putsch - a German word describing a coup or violent attempt to overthrow a government.

### R

Rallies, Rally - a political event with speakers and a crowd, designed to increase support for a politician, political party or an idea.

# GLOSSARY

Real wages - a person's income in terms of how much they can buy after taking inflation into account.

Rebellion - armed resistance against a government or leader, or resistance to other authority or control.

Rebels - people who rise in opposition or armed resistance against an established government or leader.

Reform, Reforming - change, usually in order to improve an institution or practice.

Reparations - payments made by the defeated countries in a war to the victors to help pay for the cost of and damage from the fighting.

Repress, Repression - politically, to prevent something or control people by by force.

Republic - a state or country run by elected representatives and an elected/nominated president. There is no monarch.

Revolution - the forced overthrow of a government or social system by its own people.

Right wing - a political view with beliefs centred around nationalism and a desire for an authoritarian government opposed to communism.

## S

Sabotage - to deliberately destroy, damage or obstruct, especially to gain a political or military advantage.

Scapegoat - someone who is blamed for the wrongdoings or mistakes of others.

Slavic people, Slavs - the main ethnic group of people living in Eastern Europe.

Socialist - one who believes in the principles of socialism.

Spartacists - a group of communists in Germany who staged an unsuccessful revolution in 1919.

Standard of living - level of wealth and goods available to an individual or group.

State of emergency - where a national emergency, disaster or crisis has occurred in which normal government procedures are suspended so it can deal with the situation.

State, States - an area of land or a territory ruled by one government.

Sterilisation, Sterilise - to clean something so it is free of bacteria; also refers to a medical procedure that prevents a person from being able to reproduce.

Strike - a refusal by employees to work as a form of protest, usually to bring about change in their working conditions. It puts pressure on their employer, who cannot run the business without workers.

Superior - better or higher in rank, status or quality.

Suppress, Suppression - the use of force to stop something, such as a protest.

Synagogue - a Jewish place of worship.

## T

Tactic - a strategy or method of achieving a goal.

Territorial - relating to land or territory.

Territories, Territory - an area of land under the control of a ruler/country.

Totalitarian - someone who wants a system of government in which the leader has total control, or a dictatorship, and also used to refer to that system of government.

Trade unions - organised groups of workers who cooperate to make their lives better at work. For example, they might negotiate for better pay and then organise a strike if one is refused.

Treason - the crime of betraying one's country, often involving an attempt to overthrow the government or kill the monarch.

Treasurer - the person in charge of an organisation's money or finances.

Treaty - a formal agreement, signed and ratified by two or more parties.

## U

Undesirable, Undesirables, Untermenschen - a German word meaning 'sub-human' which refers to those considered racially and/or socially inferior.

Upper class - a socio-economic group consisting of the richest people in a society who are wealthy because they own land or property.

## V

Veteran, Veterans - an ex-soldier.

## W

Working class - socio-economic group consisting of those engaged in waged labour, especially manual work or industry, who typically do not have much money.

# INDEX

## A
Adolf Hitler - *102*
Art
    Bauhaus - *42*
    Expressionism - *41*
    Modernism - *41*
    New objectivism - *41*
Art, Nazi Germany - *78*

## B
Bamberg Conference - *49*
Bauhaus - *42*
Boycott of Jewish shops - *91*

## C
Chancellor, Hitler becomes - *56*
Charles G Dawes - *96*
Concentration camps - *67*
Concordat - *70*
Culture, Weimar Republic - *39*

## D
DAF - *84*
DAP - *42*
Dawes Plan - *32*
Decree for the Protection of the People and the State - *59*
Disabled, treatment of - *89*
Drexler, Anton - *97*

## E
Ebert, Friedrich - *98*
Edelweiss Pirates - *95*
Education - *82*
Election results, 1933 - *60*
Election results, Nazi Party - *55*
Election, presidential - *55*
Enabling Act - *61*
Expressionism - *41*

## F
Film, Nazi Germany - *78*

## G
General von Schleicher - *108*
German Labour Front - *84*
German Revolution - *18*
German Workers' Party - *42*
Germany, WW1 - *16*
Gestapo - *66*
Goebbels, Joseph - *98*
Great Depression, impact on Germany - *51*
Gustav Stresemann - *109*
Gypsies, treatment of - *90*

## H
Hess, Rudolf - *99*
Heydrich, Reinhard - *100*
Himmler, Heinrich - *100*
Hindenburg, Paul von - *101*
Hitler becomes chancellor - *56*
Hitler, Adolf - *102*
Homosexuals, treatment of - *89*
Hyperinflation, Weimar Republic - *31*

## J
Jews, treatment of - *91*

## K
Kapp Putsch - *28*
Kapp, Wolfgang - *104*
Kellogg-Briand Pact - *35*
Kristallnacht - *93*

## L
Labour Front - *84*
Left-wing views - *23*
Legal system, Nazi control - *68*
Liebknecht, Karl - *104*
Locarno Pact - *33*
Ludendorff, Erich - *105*
Luxemburg, Rosa - *106*

## M
Modernism - *41*
Munich Putsch - *46*
Music - *76*

# INDEX

## N

NSDAP - *42*
Nazi Germany
   Art - *78*
   Art and Culture - *76*
   Catholics - *69*
   Education - *82*
   Establishment of dictatorship - *61*
   Film - *78*
   Literature - *75*
   Music - *76*
   Print press - *73*
   Propaganda - *72*
   Protestants - *71*
   Radio - *77*
   Rallies - *74*
   Religion - *68*
   Sport - *75*
   Standard of living - *85*
   Unemployment - *83*
   Women - *79*
   Youth - *80*
Nazi Opposition - *94*
Nazi Party - *44*
   support 1920s - *50*
   support increase - *52*
Nazi Party/reorganisation - *48*
New objectivism - *41*
Night of Broken Glass - *93*
Night of the Long Knives - *63*
Nuremburg Laws - *92*

## O

Occupation of the Ruhr - *29*
Opposition
   Edelweiss Pirates - *95*
   Swing Youth - *95*
   White Rose - *96*
Opposition to the Nazis - *94*
Owen Young - *111*

## P

Papen, Franz von - *106*
Pastors' Emergency League - *72*

Persecution - *87*
Persecution, homosexuals - *89*
Police state, creation of - *64*
Political challenges, Weimar Republic - *25*
Political violence, Weimar Republic - *26*
Presidential election - *55*
Propaganda
   Print press - *73*

## R

Radio - *77*
Rallies - *74*
Recovery, Weimar Republic - *37*
Reich Church - *71*
Reich Labour Front - *84*
Reichstag Fire - *58*
Religion
   Catholics - *69*
   Concordat - *70*
   Protestants - *71*
   Reich Church - *71*
Religion, Nazi views - *68*
Right-wing views - *24*
Rohm, Ernst - *107*
Roma, treatment of - *90*
Ruhr Occupation - *29*

## S

SA - *43*
SD - *66*
SS - *65*
Scheidemann, Philipp - *108*
Schleicher, Kurt von - *108*
Schutzstaffel - *65*
Secret police - *66*
Sicherheitsdienst des Reichsführers-SS - *66*
Spartacist Revolt - *27*
Spartacist uprising - *27*
Standard of living, Weimar Republic - *38*
Stresemann, Gustav - *109*
Sturmabteilung - *43*
Support for Nazis, limited - *50*
Swing Youth - *95*

# INDEX

## T
**Treaty of Versailles** - *22*

## U
**Unemployment** - *83*

## V
**Volksgemeinschaft** - *73*
**Von Papen, Franz** - *106*

## W
**WWI, Germany** - *16*
**Weimar**
    **Bauhaus movement** - *42*
    **Culture** - *39*
    **Expressionism in art** - *41*
    **Hyperinflation** - *31*
    **League of Nations** - *34*
    **Modernism in art** - *41*
    **New objectivism in art** - *41*
    **Standard of Living** - *38*
    **Women** - *38*
**Weimar Republic** - *18*
**Weimar/Political challenges** - *25*
**Weimar/Political violence** - *26*
**Weimar/Recovery** - *37*
**White Rose group** - *96*
**Wilhelm II, Kaiser of Germany** - *110*
**Women, Nazi Germany** - *79*
**Women, Weimar Republic** - *38*

## Y
**Young Plan** - *36*
**Youth** - *80*